LEAVING
the BOUGH

International Publishers, New York

LEAVING
the BOUGH

50 AMERICAN POETS OF THE 80s

Edited by Roger Gaess

Library of Congress Cataloging in Publication Data

Main entry under title:

Leaving the bough.

   1. American poetry—20th century. I. Gaess,
Roger, 1943-
PS615.L37   811'.54'08   81-20087
ISBN 0-7178-0592-1   AACR2
ISBN 0-7178-0587-5 (pbk.)

Acknowledgments and Copyright Notices

The poems in this anthology are protected by copyright and may not be reproduced in any form without the consent of the poets, their publishers, or their representatives. Thanks are due for permission to include the following poems.

AI: "Pentecost" from *Killing Floor* by Ai, Copyright © 1979 by Ai. Reprinted by permission of Houghton Mifflin Company. "Conversation" first published in the *Paris Review.*

ALIESAN, JODY: "sutra blues or, this pain is bliss" and "radiation leak" from *as if it will matter* by Jody Aliesan, Copyright © 1978 by Jody Aliesan. Reprinted by permission of The Seal Press and the author. "Arachne" from *Soul Claiming* by Jody Aliesan, Copyright © 1975 by Jody Aliesan. Reprinted by permission of Mulch Press and the author.

ANDERSON, TERESA: "Our People" and "Delphine" from *Speaking in Sign* (West End Press) by Teresa Anderson, Copyright © 1978 by Teresa Anderson.

BENNETT, BRUCE: "The Bad Apple" from *Apple: An Anthology of Upstate New York Poets* (State Street Press), edited by Judith Kitchen. "Success Story" and "The Stick" printed by permission of the author.

BERNADINE: "a letter from when," "an open letter-poem-note to Vincent van G.," and "it begins softly" from *It Begins Softly* (Women for Racial and Economic Equality) by Bernadine, Copyright © 1980 by Bernadine.

BERSSENBRUGGE, MEI-MEI: "The Membrane" (first published in *Partisan Review*, Vol. XLII, No. 1), "Sleep," and "The Translation of Verver" (first appeared in *Partisan Review*, Vol. XLV, No. 3) from *Random Possession* by Mei-mei Berssenbrugge, Copyright © 1979 by Mei-mei Berssenbrugge. Reprinted by permission of I. Reed Books.

BLAZEK, DOUGLAS: "My Definition of Poetry" from *Exercises in Memorizing Myself* (Twowindows Press) by Douglas Blazek, Copyright © 1976 by Douglas Blazek. "Eichmann" from *Skull Juices* (Twowindows Press) by Douglas Blazek, Copyright © 1970 by Douglas Blazek. "Greed" originally appeared in *Skywriting*, Copyright © 1974 by *Skywriting*.

*F*or Jacquie and Angelika

& my special thanks to Terry Hegarty, Michael McMath, and Gareth Esersky, who read and commented at various stages; to Louis Diskin, for his continued editorial efforts; and, of course, to all those poets who warmly contributed to these pages; and my sincere apologies to the numerous poets who deserved to be included and, through no fault of their own, were not.

Contents

Early Words, Early Warnings

i.

Poetry is a high-risk calling. A voice speaks urgently about the serious confusion of life, that is, about those cries of joy or of distress which command us all during the moments we are most alive. But, unlike the poet, who must be a risk-taker, the poem itself needs a protective covering, a form that not only reflects its content but helps to preserve it. Yet form should never be the primary justification for the poem, though ideally it is a pleasure in itself.

I seek a poetry that is an extension of the poet's vulnerable and highly receptive sensibility, that is not satisfied with the common, and that enables me to live more fully. However, a majority of the currently respectable poets and critics carry an anti-emotional prejudice. And most readers have been trained to seek entertainment rather than emotion, to seek poems that amuse rather than move, that inspire forgetfulness rather than remembrance. The mass consumption of art promoted at present furthers only the type of art that can easily be consumed, and in turn the passivity of the consumer is encouraged.[1] This may in part account for the "difficulty" of much of the best poetry, for the poetry that I value invites the reader's complicity and commitment. Unfortunately, in a culture of standardized response dominated by popular conceptions of creativity, poetry means poetry for the few, for poetry must remain without effect on any audience that fears "the real thing."

Some poetry is necessarily "difficult" due to the very nature of what it is: a thing of heightened consciousness (Marianne Moore) in which language is used in a way that (to borrow a phrase of Gerard Manley Hopkins) is "counter, original, spare, strange." The poem refines and humanizes both the poet and the reader. The poet gives up part of his or her life in order to arrive at an intense expression of feeling, while in turn the reader is made aware that something matters, and will never again feel the same about that particular thing. The best poems may become part of the reader's spiritual life and free readers from some of the prisons of their everyday lived experiences, thereby contributing to the formation of a more unified personality. They might, like Hesse's Knulp, bring "the settled folk a little homesickness for freedom." But readers must respond with the whole of their being, just as the poet has earlier done. The more the readers attempt to enter the concentrated life of the poem, the more they are forced to come to terms with themselves.

For a century or more a dangerous notion has circulated that poetry is a luxury, or a beautiful alternative to living. It was not the Industrial Revolution itself but a particular assumption gratuitously accompanying it that brought this about—the assumption that culture comes after the problems of industrialization are settled, rather than concurrently. It was—and by many still is—thought wasteful and selfish to turn to the transformation offered by poetry until everyone's "basic needs" have been met. Such an attitude divides the human spirit and isolates culture and the imagination from the other essential workings of society, thereby determining not only the isolation of the poet but the impoverishment of society as well. For no society that minimizes human emotional response can ever approximate sanity and justice. Unfortunately, in contemporary America, both the poet and the reader are continually confronted by a culture that regards poetry as alien, useless, or effete. In such an environment, a belief in poetry is difficult to sustain. A generation ago, Stephen Spender, at a time when he was deeply involved in a consideration of poetry's social role, wondered somewhat pessimistically, "Perhaps we can only achieve our own transformation, inside ourselves, but with the possibility of communicating the secret to a happy few."[2]

The question of audience is implied in the Romantic extremes of outward and inward transformation: Shelley's insistence that poets are the unacknowledged legislators; Keat's lamentation, "O for a life of sensations rather than of thoughts!" Every poet anticipates a somewhat different audience according to the particular assumptions and hopes he or she maintains. Certainly Shelley, who hoped that poetry would incite people to fashion a more just world, anticipated a different audience than Keats.

Not that the contemporary poet consciously sets out to change society. Too much has happened in the past century and a half for any poet of today to proceed on that assumption. Nevertheless, it is an assumption here that any poet speaking honestly and forcefully in the form of a poem, speaks to others of transformation. No matter how stagnant a society, there is always an interchange between the outward and inward realms. Just as the long-term fate of the individual cannot be considered apart from the significant events of wider society, neither is social progress possible without inward transformation. Without the transformation of both, the other is of severely limited value. If revolutions are grounded in insights into the human condition (as I think they are), the best poems are truly revolutionary.

Of course, for poetry to fulfill Shelley's vision, the politician-planner and the poet could not inhabit intellectually exclusive worlds. Poetry would not merely concern itself with the great range of human issues, it would also inform political decision-making. As Thomas Mann remarked in the early 1930s, "Karl Marx must read Friedrich Hölderlin." The "affirming flame" of passionate commitment must light both ways.

ii.

Around the close of the decade of the 1950s, three influential anthologies appeared. *New Poets of England and America* (World, 1957), edited by Donald Hall, Robert Pack, and Louis Simpson, brought together some of the more formal poetry of the fifties. Not long after, Donald Allen edited a stylistically freer collection of contemporary poetry, *The New American Poetry, 1945-1960* (Grove, 1960). A third selection, *Poets of Today* (International, 1962), edited by Walter Lowenfels, offered a socially-conscious point of view and represented racial and ethnic minorities and progressive writers beyond the tokenism that had characterized previous general anthologies. Together the three anthologies presented the full range of American poetry then being written.

The contrast offered by the Hall-Pack-Simpson and Allen collections was pronounced enough to set off a short-termed "war of the anthologies": the "academic" or "Establishment" or "cooked" vs. the "raw" or "beat" or "Underground," as they variously have been known. Of course their real differences originated as much in life style as in poetic style, though certainly neither is exclusive of the other. Since the two wings delineated by these anthologies still exist, the resulting implications cannot be ignored.

One wing is thought of as the Establishment or academic largely because those poets who compose it usually hold positions as editors, critics (or reviewers), or university professors, much in the way that Wallace Stevens had been a corporate director. A good deal of the time of many of these poets is spent administering poetry. They often determine what poetry is widely seen and heard through their influence on grants, prizes, fellowships, publication, publicity, public readings, recordings, teaching appointments, and other forms of financial disbursement. Their criteria for quality is an extension of the safe positions they hold and there tends to be little at stake in either their lives or the poetry they write or value. They implicitly defend traditional rather than radical concepts of content and form. Though occasionally critical of the status quo, they write from the standpoint of those who maintain good social standing, whose preferences have been shaped by those who hold power.

The academic poets display a thorough knowledge of literature and a marked technical competence. They regularly publish in the well-financed (or well-funded) literary periodicals. But their environment and interests generally revolve around "the poetry business." For the most part, they reject an open encounter with magnitude and mystery in such forms as suffering, hunger, ecstasy, loneliness, ethical alternatives, or the good and evil within us all. Their knowledge has largely been acquired from books rather than experience. Having rarely participated in that direct acquisition of knowledge, the concern and voice of such poets is consequently limited because the mind behind it never directly learned to experience feelings. ("The insight must be earned as much as the poem," Jack Gilbert once wisely insisted.)[3] The reader is justified in asking whether the vision of such poets can be relied upon in matters of real consequence. It is in this context also that we might wonder about the ultimate value of the now widespread university-level creative writing programs—which are usually administered by such poets—and the "instant poets" they tend to produce.

Of course it should not be assumed that any poet who works in an academic setting is necessarily an academic poet. A more precisely distinguishing feature of this kind of poet is his or her propensity toward careerism. A typical poetry career is shaped along the following lines. First, acquire an initial power base, such as the editorship of a slick literary magazine. Inevitably, other poet-editors will publish your work with the "unstated" understanding that their own work would receive extra consideration regarding eventually finding its way into *your* magazine. Through mutual favors such as these, your reputation will be quickly promoted. Jobs based on reputation, and on the "major-house" book publication that also might follow from it, are easily forthcoming from universities. And your academic tenure is secured through continued regular publication of poems—poems of usually minimum quality. Obviously these pressures of careerism necessitate that Delmore Schwartz's sound advice—"one ought to write as much as possible and publish as little as possible"—goes unheeded. The imagination of necessity is opposed by the necessity of imagination. The spontaneity grounded in need and experience assumes a position of relative unimportance.

These poets are usually far more concerned about their careers as poets than about writing good poetry. Their goal is to keep their names regularly in print. The number involved in "the poetry hustle" is large enough for the grants-awards process to operate in much the same way as the publication process. The same people are singled out for awards and for sitting on committees that determine the distribution of awards. The rules of the game keep healthy a small number of influential and self-perpetuating cliques. Thus lies the new road to the Pulitzer.

But the academics have not cornered the market in poetry careers. Members of the other wing dominating contemporary poetry—which is variously called the Underground or "alternate poetry," or by a particular group label—occasionally maintain a careerist stance as well, though even in such instances their connection with direct experience is usually not lost. They might be referred to as "bohemian" but, given their cliquishness, they are more correctly bohemians with club houses. They publish their own magazines, the pages of which are usually limited to the work of their friends and their friends' friends. Their work tends toward the experimental. In contrast to the technically competent, well-mannered, and largely irrelevant poetry of the academics, most of the Underground poets misuse their energy and experience on frivolous or shock or self-indulgent poems that are technically rough. Sometimes they write notes to friends on matters of fairly mundane concern and pass these off as poetry. The work of most of these writers exhibits a quality of "easy reading," often being a poetry turned out on the run, a poetry sketched.

Thus the American poetry-reading public is relatively inundated by academic and Underground poetry. For the reader the question becomes "Must I choose between the two?" The question should not be asked casually. In the process of reading manuscripts for this collection, when I asked (in the tradition of the Lowenfels anthology) for active poetry of involvement and commitment which implied that something was as stake in the poet's life, few contributors understood what I meant, though some of the most widely-published poets submitted manuscripts.

That the best-known poets are necessarily the best is a hard illusion to dispel in our market-oriented culture. But, as mentioned earlier, reputations have been inflated. With few exceptions, for each poet published by a "major" house, there are several more-talented and more-relevant under-known ones. As David Kirby expressed in *The New Republic:* Two groups "exist: the vast number of talentless poets who publish and promote themselves because no one will do it for them, and the several dozen name poets who live mainly in the northeast, who are published by New York and Boston firms, and who are nearly as immune from meaningful criticism as the first group thanks to a protective circle of critics. . . . But between these two is a third group of perhaps 100 poets who . . . eventually place their books with small independent presses or university presses. This is where the most interesting writing comes from."[4] In assembling this anthology, it was largely from this latter group that I drew.

Of course the establishment houses' publication of serious poetry should not be condemned; they should be publishing more of it. Many small presses have been thriving (especially during the last decade) because of the commercialism and irresponsibility of the large presses. Until the "major" houses move away from their academic or "popular" standards, the small publishers will continue to provide the more authentic printed forum for contemporary American poetry.

iii.

By their very nature, anthologies offer poets apart from their complete body of work. Anyone reading only anthologies would be missing a great deal, yet so would anyone who read only current literary magazines or recent individual collections. To attempt to rate these three ways of poetry in order of importance would be a mistake, but an anthology is a good starting place for someone coming to poetry.

The acquired skill of appreciating modern poetry is in part an ability to recognize a poem's alternatives: what the poet's concern is and how that concern is (or is not) realized in the poem—i.e. how syntax, diction, tone, rhythm, line, association, atmosphere, form, ambiguity, etc. may be utilized to crystallize the intensity of a particular attitude. A familiarity with the recent past is perhaps indispensable: movements, schools, tendencies since World War II; as well as a general understanding of Modernism, its roots and influences. After a while, discerning readers will acquire a feel for where to turn next in their reading, and the quest for historical perspective will certainly lead to the poetry of other countries and other languages, for U.S. poetry has become international in this century, and the influence of translations has been enormous (largely because experience has become international).

After the relatively new reader of poetry has become somewhat familiar with the alternatives open to a poet, that reader might turn his or her attention to the work of one or two particular poets in order to examine development as well as influences. And, furthermore, there are a few dozen "little" and other literary magazines offering worthwhile recent poetry.

Every good poem encompasses considerably more than its explicit meanings. Occasionally the aural qualities provide the key to a poem's emotional level. A great many recordings of poetry are now available in the best libraries and record shops. At the very least, try to imagine how a poem sounds to the ear while reading it with the eye. Or, better still, read the poem out loud. The point, really, is to gain as wide a perspective as possible with which to yield the poem's most complete meaning(s). Stay with difficult poetry until you can walk around inside it: many of the best poems demand several readings. And go in search of those few poets who offer a vitality particularly interesting and relevant to you; discover those few poets whose poetry rings with an immediacy (evokes a need). Nothing is more exciting for a reader than encountering a poet who speaks with a voice that reverberates.

iv.

All editors are a product and ultimately a prisoner of their own prejudices and preferences, and, for that reason alone, it should be incumbent upon them to set forth their objectives and values. In general, I followed the advice of Paul Carroll, who, in his "Note about the Selection" to *The Young American Poets* (Follett, 1968), outlined, "Include only those poets who seem genuine and exciting; and include only those poems or that one poem by each writer which you admire without reservation."

To attempt to explain what "genuine and exciting" mean to me: In the process of reading manuscripts, I looked for poems of involvement, relevancy, commitment, and immediacy rather than of detachment or self-indulgence. I needed to feel that something was at stake in the poem and in the life that initiated it. I avoided the safe poetry of light academic verse (a current vogue) or of calm disillusionment or of high-tone rhetoric in the form of still-life delicacy and tediously observed detail, the order of which has been the standard poetry of the *New Yorker* in recent years. I carried the impression that the latter poetry presented a part of the *nature* of experience but not the *force* of it. I tried to counter the current anti-emotional orthodoxy by presenting serious (though certainly not grim) poetry of intense language and emotional outpouring, that is coupled with the surprise offered by a new way of seeing. Whether a poet adopted an experimental or traditional form was, for me, of minor relative importance. And I could "admire without reservation" poetry which exhibits a content of consequence as well as a technical proficiency, for I believe that content is an integral part of valuable poetry.

Obviously an anthology is limited by an individual (editorial) perception: every editor is affected by moods and myriad outside and personal influences, but these have their positive as well as negative implications. Ultimately, and fortunately, the poetry always speaks for itself.

A few words about my method of selection. In order to follow a process of open submission, ads requesting manuscripts were run in *Coda* and a number of other periodicals. Several hundred manuscripts were received in response to these notices. About sixty additional poets were invited to submit as well. The selection process was a long, arduous one extending over many months. Every submission was read closely. I found my criteria for acceptance being altered somewhat as the readings progressed. On more than one occasion, I recalled (and later accepted) work that had initially been returned.

My original plan was to include only poets under 40, but eventually exceptions were made and "younger" came to mean "under 45." I decided not to turn away from vital poetry merely because a contributor had somewhat outdistanced an arbitrary nativity date. Nor do I share the opinion that poets necessarily "strike their note long before forty"; Thomas Hardy did not challenge attention as a poet until he was nearly sixty.

Presented here are a wide range of individual voices that indicate the diversity of writing cultures contributing to our national poetry. Some of the poets have published in only a few literary magazines, while others have had several books of poetry published. Poems of social consciousness will be found next to poetry of inner concern in a complementary way that has possibly never happened before. Though the overwhelming majority of these poets are independent of movements, they nevertheless embody important tendencies. (Perhaps one ground for judging an anthology's significance is whether or not it effectively indicates a transition from one era into the next.) The disparate voices joined in these pages form a multi-vision anthology in a dawn of cultural interchange.

Conventional responses to work by a poet who happens to be a member of a minority group must now—more than ever before—be discouraged. Such responses inhibit the imagination of the reader. As Duane Niatum pointed out in his essay "On Stereotypes," "artists, no matter where they come from, use some images and symbols that are uniquely their own. And what is remarkable about the symbol with a soul is that it calls to us no matter where we started from."[5] In recognition of the general uselessness of relatively arbitrary grouping, contributors are presented here in alphabetical order.

Leaving the Bough simply attempts to present an entire range of human experience—the overall impression of what it's like to be alive in the America of today and of the recent past. Occasionally the lines may hint at confusion, that particular confusion that comes from a lived point of view, but what serious poet has not found the world confusing, mysterious, and wonder-full? Perhaps this anthology will find its way into the hands of someone embarking on an overnight train ride . . . and will offer that reader a trip into strange and previously dangerous foreign territory.

ROGER GAESS

Notes:

1. Günter Kunert, "Paradox as a Principle," *New German Critique* (Fall 1976): 137.

2. Stephen Spender, "Inside the Cage: Reflections on Conditioned and Unconditioned Imagination," in *English Critical Essays: Twentieth Century,* Second Series, ed. Derek Hudson (London: Oxford University Press, 1958), p. 268.

3. I would here like to gratefully acknowledge my debt to the poetry and prose of Jack Gilbert, which were directly or indirectly the source of several ideas expressed in section ii.

4. *The New Republic,* 16 December 1978, p. 3.

5. Duane Niatum, "On Stereotypes," *Parnassus: Poetry in Review* 7, no. 1 (Fall/ Winter 1978): 164-65.

LEAVING
the BOUGH

Ai

PENTECOST

For Myself

Rosebud Morales, my friend,
before you deserted,
you'd say anyone can kill an Indian
and forget it the same instant,
that it will happen to me, Emiliano Zapata.
But my men want more corn for tortillas,
more pigs, more chickens, more chilis
and land.
If I haven't got a gun or a knife,
I'll fight with a pitchfork or a hoe,
to take them from the bosses,
those high-flying birds,
with the pomade glistening on their hair,
as they promenade into their coffins.
And if I'm killed, if we're all killed right now,
we'll go on, the true Annunciation.

Rosebud, how beautiful this day is.
I'm riding to meet Guajardo.
He'll fight with me now,
against Carranza.
When I get to the hacienda, it's quiet.
Not many soldiers,
a sorrel horse, its reins held
by a woman in a thin, white American dress
and Guajardo standing on a balcony.

I get off my horse and start up the steps.
My legs burn, my chest,
my jaw, my head.
There's a hill in front of me;

it's slippery, I have to use my hands to climb it.
At the top, it's raining fire and blood
on rows and rows of black corn.
Machetes are scattered everywhere.
I grab one and start cutting the stalks.
When they hit the ground,
they turn into men.
I yell at them.
You're damned in the cradle,
in the grave, even in Heaven.
Dying doesn't end anything.
Get up. Swing those machetes.
You can't steal a man's glory
without a goddamned fight.
Boys, take the land, take it; it's yours.
If you suffer in the grave,
you can kill from it.

CONVERSATION

For Robert Lowell

We smile at each other
and I lean back against the wicker couch.
How does it feel to be dead? I say.
You touch my knees with your blue fingers.
And when you open your mouth,
a ball of yellow light falls to the floor
and burns a hole through it.
Don't tell me, I say. I don't want to hear.
Did you ever, you start,
wear a certain kind of silk dress
and just by accident,
so inconsequential you barely notice it,
your fingers graze that dress
and you hear the sound of a knife cutting paper,
you see it too
and you realize how that image

is simply the extension of another image,
that your own life is a chain
of words
that one day will snap.
Words, you say, young girls in a circle, holding hands
and beginning to rise heavenward
like white, helium balloons
in their confirmation dresses,
the wreaths of flowers on their heads spinning
and above all that,
that's where I'm floating, Florence,
and that's what it's like
only ten times clearer,
ten times more horrible.
Could anyone alive survive it?

Jody Aliesan

ARACHNE

She was a weaver.
What she made was too perfect
for the gods to bear.
They were jealous, like her teachers.
They ripped her cloth.
She hanged herself.
They turned her into a spider.

I see spiders everywhere:
hanging dead in their cobwebs,
racing for cover across the floor.

Last night
one floated past me on the bathwater
and here's another,
pale and careful,
climbing over warp ties on my loom.
They're harmless,
but they distract me

and I make mistakes.

SUTRA BLUES
            OR, THIS PAIN IS BLISS

I blow ashes into the hearth
hoarsely, with a long breath
as if the curls were your hair.

the old rhythm of wanting you
teases me into dancing
alone on this gray fall day
dancing to some slow smoulder blues;

coming on with the taste of this ache
it tempts me out of detachment
behind the backs of the angels

and we moan with a smile,
the rhythm and me,
we both know yes suffering comes
from holding on, from wanting,
it comes from desire

and we both know release from pain
comes from
letting
go.

RADIATION LEAK

I come from farm folk:
we know about trouble,
settle near a stream
in case the well runs dry,
plant enough to store
so we'll eat through the winter.
we learn about the signs of spring,
how to watch the sky.

but the radio says
all our food jars are poison.
everywhere. overnight.
don't touch them at all.
and the stream only looks clear;
you can't see the death in it.
if you drank a cup of it
you'd rot from inside.

helicopters came,
people in them wearing space suits.
they dropped us food pills, books
on how to stay alive.
waves on the lakeshore
slap up with fishbellies.
evergreen needles
are turning yellow,
needles and feathers falling

I hold my head in my hands
and bring away hair.

Teresa Anderson

OUR PEOPLE

For more years than I can remember,
the crops have failed,
in this land where rain is a fugitive;
and the people in my blood have
lived in houses cut from the earth.

In summer children here have
always made music from the
rhythm of the long days,
and the women in my veins
have learned to make banquets
from meagre tables.

More than once in spring blizzards
the cattle have been lost,
and more than once the winter-born
child, in a room with no stove,
has died at the breast.

Yet we have been more than survivors;
all the best I will ever be
lies rooted in the earth
where my grandmother sleeps,
on a prairie swept clean of trees,
under harsh, cloudless sky,
where wheat flows in waves
over the first sod houses,
and the dust of the dead
sings under the blade of the plow.

DELPHINE

In every direction from here
the land is flat and merciless,
horizons painfully stark,
trees spaced wide apart
and ponds too often dry;
Louis Desaire chose a cruel
and inconstant homestead,
known for blizzards and
duststorms, locusts and
withering blight in the wheat;
his children have headed for
the certainty of towns,
abandoning the farm to the
windmill dismantled, the
well overgrown with sunflowers
and the front porch sagging
under the weight of a sleeping cat.
Delphine's kitchen is used as a
feed shed for cattle who have
broken in the door, and the
iron stove is now a nesting
place for prairie hens and mice;
thistle-topped grasses cover the cellar
out back, and the barn has long since
lost its battle with searing winds.
But at night when the house shifts
under the flying shadows of clouds,
they come back, the man
with his bawdy laugh,
hands reaching for
sweet, home-made wine
and eyes following the
woman, a diminutive,
green-eyed girl now,
just come from the wedding dance,
who stands uncertainly at
the parlor door, wondering

at the crude sound of his English,
picturing a cradle by the stove
and wishing he would remove
the pins from her heavy, dark hair.

Damar, Kansas

Bruce Bennett

THE BAD APPLE

The peasant with the black tooth. The
crone who tried to core him. The boys who
played keepaway. How he was flung to a
horse. How he lay in a ditch, water swirling,
but stuck fast . . . Then, blunt fingers;
burlap; darkness.

It wouldn't be long before they found
him, pocked skin, flesh flaking. Where was
the sense? Why had he been spared?

With a rush it came: the mouth, the
hoof, the knife. Soaring. Those hours in the water.
Listen, he cried.

Listen!

The ruddy, perfect apples cut short
their dreaming.

He began to speak.

SUCCESS STORY

A man had nothing to write about.

So he wrote about having nothing to write about.

People with nothing to think about liked what he wrote.

He gained fame.

He went on tour and read before large audiences. Thousands lined up to hear him.

He began to be imitated.

Critics with nothing to talk about argued about his influence.

He won awards.

He appeared on programs and was described as a "phenomenon".

He granted interviews.

He became "a spokesman for his era".

Historians named that era after him.

They discussed what he represented.

It gave them something to write about.

THE STICK

A man picked up a stick, which felt
strange to his hand. He tapped the ground.
A stream bubbled up.

He struck a rock, which split; a bird
flew out, singing.

He studied the stick; then, touched
it to his forehead. He sank into sleep.

He dreamed he was a stick, picked up
by a man. He wanted to tell how he was
a man too. "If I perform miracles," he
thought, "he'll know I'm not a stick."

So he made water bubble up; a bird
fly out of a rock. But the man tossed
him aside.

He woke, and looked around: there
was no stream; the rock was whole.

He couldn't find the stick.

Bernadine

A LETTER FROM WHEN

"Tomorrow" it said
the envelope was addressed to
"Tomorrow" . . . it was under my door
and for many moments I was
afraid, for its paper
was a white turned yellow become brown and
almost burned by a time perhaps no longer living,
while its ink had faded tha words to almost
whispers   and I was afraid
because I didn't want to disturb tha signature of
Death . . .   but, no,
no, of course not. I mean, when I managed to read it I
found that the unknown writer
had written of something other
and quite the opposite . . .

so I share this with you,
this that America speaks of only
in tha voice of silence.
please note:
this letter is reprinted in full
and exactly as originally worded.
tha writer titled it,

So my country could feel the sun

    I was a worker
because I like to build.
I was a worker-soldier because,
well . . . how can I explain to you
my love for children
and my need to build . . .
I was a worker-soldier because
my country is so young
and we had to have tomorrow . . .

but what I gave was not much,
though it couldn't have been more.

but the land is fertile, you see,
and flowers would
cover what remained
and the rains gently
would wash dried blood
and the flesh
blown from our bodies would give this
soil new seed to grow
(and please know, try to understand
that our land loves the rain).
our bones would be buried here and later
we would be honored—
you see, there wasn't always time
then . . .
     yesterday
would account for now and no one
would forget,
no one would not remember
the pain
the dignity
the land,
this land that is fertile,
on which tomorrows are built.

you see,
we defended our freedom then so the Revolution,
it would yet live,
and the children
they would grow. . . .

              Sincerely,
               A worker-soldier
               in the company of millions.
               Leningrad, 1941

P.S. Please send this to others
because the truth can know no ownership.

AN OPEN LETTER-POEM-NOTE TO VINCENT VAN G.

they were buying . . . your name maybe
but you weren't at the auction to sell it and I'm
trying to understand, to figure out
exactly what part of you they want to possess while they
buy power over things and some people and
positions in high places they
say you're good investment and I
don't understand . . . were they
buying your need to work, your desire to give were they
buying your pain, your personal problems because
they're damn sure you were crazy did they
bid in tha millions because you
wouldn't've wanted it and didn't paint for that reason
(but then   folks like us have to remember
money has its own morals and never listens to
tha "lowly") were they
buying your ability, your "magic" as some say because they
want to understand an art misunderstood did they
think feeling could be bought and measured in $bills were they
trying to buy yours I . . . really don't know . . . were they
trying to buy you back into life when they
care so little for tha living do they
want to examine your eyes and explain
how you saw what you saw and painted what you felt I
really,   really don't know,

knowing I know too little about it: tha stuff of buying, selling.
but if you were to ask me I
could say a lot about small things and a bit about large matters.
For instance, I know what a penny looks like and what it won't
buy while I forget whose face is on a quarter . . . but that's because
I see it only occasionally and it leaves
so quickly. . . . I can tell you, too, about a dollar bill, which is
soft-like and so crumpled because it's passed thru a million
hands like mine and everytime I touch it I can feel how
we've used it countless times to pay ourselves out of some problems
we hope . . . I can also describe to you tha contorted mouths of
hungry faces and what no money will do.

Now these are tha things I can say with certainty. These
be tha things I understand . . .

myFriend,
they're trying to take tha life that was yours from you, like
when they take tha cause from tha speaker, tha deed from tha doer,
tha work from tha worker, then sell what they've done like
money means a heartbeat—but of course we know they know nothing
of life . . .

If it were appropriate I'd apologize for what they've done, but
they been doin' it long and they're doin' it still and there's
no time for bein' sorry for what I didn't do anyway. You see,
I'm a member of tha Resistance & Reconstruction movement. We
fought yesterday and we're fighting now, fighting because we
know with our lives that art and so much else belongs to us.
Such are tha ways of this war and its truth . . .

Vincent, eventhough tha war goes slowly right now, please know
its final resting place will be found in our victory. Of this
we are sure . . .

   Titled "Le Jardin du Poete, Arles," 1888, Van Gogh painted it as a celebra-
tion of his friendship with the artist Paul Gauguin.
   In the fifth month of this twentieth century's '80, it was bought by the
highest bidder for 5.2 million dollars.

IT BEGINS SOFTLY

it begins inside first
when finally
we've learned to question and grow
and grow to love
and learned to give giving
a great deal more   than hope;
it begins when we've understood
that tomorrow needs
every atom of strength   now;

it starts
when we've committed ourselves
selfishly
and selflessly
to tha forces of life.
   it's the fetus inside we have
   no choice
   except
   to feel it grow
   to aid its coming

and tha revolution begins
just this softly

Mei-mei Berssenbrugge

THE MEMBRANE

In lower orders up to the mammal
a membrane
with its terribly narrow third dimension
still passed equally in both directions
The cargo itself changed
You could still believe
writhing through its tight reticulations
you might return, almost yourself
if you were strong enough
like a hero
but this next one is perfect
It takes everything in and uses it

perfectly, with no communication
Oh sometime in your sleep
on a dark night you might press your hand
toward a cool sheet
and brush against it like the womb wall
and be burned
That remains as a heavy ignorance the next day
or you might kill something
with your car when you are tired

When a thing leaves us
it no longer knows us
We miss it by the shape our senses
impress from habit into the rooms
where we hear it breathing
We're mad it knows something
now like a big voice or a sea
or the spider in front of the membrane
When a dead thing cuddles into its grave
like a minute we pity ourselves
cancel our myths

SLEEP

The animal sleeps and dreams
of something desired in the day
eyes slackened inward, tracking
in a bright world. Each limb
quivers to its own delicate rhythm
the nostrils, the abdomen. Yearning
each day sweetens the dream, but makes
it harder to wake and beach your desire
Running by the river helps, a gross
mime of subtler won races. Still
there's a resemblance. Each night
the oscillating gold wires, our bodies
glint with leaps in a lighted meadow

where smoke begins to waft through grasses
We love our own heaviness, anticipation
If I could burn my desire with kerosene
sweeten the fire with cedar shavings
and turn the meadow out—
but it is already too misty or smoky
It is getting to be always just before dawn
an empty sky, shadowy with consummations

THE TRANSLATION OF VERVER

A roan lizard writhing on a dead leaf
is the pulse, but the flash of wings is unknown
as what the first faith rests on, its color
and degree of translucence, or whether the cry
is a bird's or human, though the beat is drums
the hue of one feather, and a rooster's dreaming
before dawn is common in our language, as quarrels
in the night, what you call "random possession"
Randomness, what it rests on. By morning
the green lizard shakes a new palm leaf
That we can still hold the light like sea shells
our chance, is first faith, and repeat
the spiral swirl of a fallen blossom on the path
the salmon color fading, a new one falling
Each a god's descent to the papery music of wind
sweeping away dry ones in a rainless summer
as if the hue of the next feather were the shedding

Petionville, Haiti

Douglas Blazek

EICHMANN

He came to shut
off the gas and
electricity today.

His head loose
like a bad light fixture
his eyes gray
the color of headstones.

He was going
to shut it off
even if I lived
in an iron lung.

"I am only doing my job,"
he said.
"It means nothing
you can't pay."

"It means nothing
this life in you
mating with itself
like constant sex."

His company makes only
chest medals and bone ash
yet he wanted the money.

He wanted sixty-six dollars
and fifteen cents
but all I could do was
stare at him as if
he were the universe.

MY DEFINITION OF POETRY

I do not want
to be beautiful.
I want
to be a bathtub.

Notice the use
I would get, people
would not want
to be through with me.

Or keep me
under protective covering.

And
I would never worry
about ceremony.

Always I would
contain warm flesh.

Always I would
be functional.

Always the truth
would disrobe before me.
Always I would acquire
its perfectly realized
experience.

GREED

Far out at sea it can be seen . . .
a bull snorting through the water
its size is a city, its density is pain
armor flesh thick as technology

rumbling toward the residents on
every inconsequential American street
and when it finally crashes through our
livingroom walls it will not hand
us a dictionary or an eyeglass
it will devour us like a mouthful of grass
and our screams will be green saliva
and our lives will be digested by enzymes
in the belly of this eyeless creature
whose sinew conspired from our sperm

Olga Broumas

ELEGY

Somebody left the world last night, I felt it
so, last minute, last half breath before the storm
that hit all night last night drew back. Mid-morning
windows streaked with mud like sides of cars. How long

the journey? Sails, the windowpanes the black
thick tarp that kept the woodpile. Dry
southern wind, in minutes clothes bone-hard, clamped
to the line. Clouds heaving in. The sky, the sky, who did arrive

to kiss the eye behind the windswept sheet? Who was it, solo
no longer, shy and desirous to be clean? What song
arose, what crust between the lids
spat and forgot? I woke, my fingers in my eyes

lifted and kissed
the yellow ash, so close.

EPITHALAMION

Our mound of earth dug up
      for a new sidewalk
is as graceful as the dunes we drive to see.
      The seen
dwarfs our scale, we feel it
      tugging at our brow

and bow
      like guests in it, yet we
for bending are allowed to
      sing
some blonde dune's surface.
      We believe what we see

through the image is the song
      at its source
and so assume the world
      love, shares our intelligence
of heart, the natural
      hug, the quick kiss overturned. The smug

like their smiles more than what makes them
      smile:
white cows in November meadows
      in the galactic ravines.
Venus enters the bull at birth and again at will.
      A door shuts twice.

The twelve rings of the night, outposts
      reefs, pockets of great abandon, what
we expected poetry to be
      as children, yield. As women
we are beautiful for remembering
      how to relax all force

in an unmeasured field.
      The moment heals.

Out past where the shale you think is
            going to hold and doesn't
silverfish leap from the water
            tears are worlds not seen.

Thomas Brush

LETTER FROM THE STREET

Morning. And the alleys give up
The darkness without a sound. The half-spilled moon
Still glows at mid-day. I wonder why?
No matter. The Mission opens to smoke
And soup, and lies wrapped in newsprint.
I take another turn. The wine
Is warm and thick as July. I remember
Towns like this, dust and a blank sky, stores
Boarded up. The badlands are behind me, or balanced
In my hands like the bottle I pass
To Willy No Legs. Beyond me on ruined wood
The price of sleep is 50 cents.

                              The river is winding
Down, clogged with ice and mud, rust,
Dead things. If only I could shovel the past
Away like snow. That would be something.
There's another country in front of me
That has pockets, and a face
Full of death. The black stars
Are broken glass.

            Good-bye.

THE HAPPY POEM

If this is what we've all been
Waiting for, the ghost grinning at us over the warm afternoon,
Or smiling up from the morning
Paper, or something laughing and running
Toward us from the middle of the haunted wood, then how
Can we cope with our children
Painting their faces
Across the raining windows, and why
Do we keep seeing a bridge burst into flames
Beneath us or ourselves bursting
Into tears? And why do we despair of our wives
Who walk by themselves through the dark
Center of night, and why must we fall,
With the good-byes hardly off our lips, on some institution's hideous,
Gray bed? As now, with snow
To our knees we continue
To open doors, looking for laughter and the light
Clothing of joy, forever expecting the happy birds
Coming home to roost.

Siv Cedering

TO THE MAN WHO WATCHES SPIDERS

They say we devour our men
after mating.
But you who have watched us
for hours and days,
defend us. Some say

that women who die in childbirth
become spiders that hang in the heavens,
funerary escorts of a dying sun,
while they wait for the day
when they can devour all

of mankind. Tell them,
tell them that we, like women,
know perfection, that we lose it,
quickly, that we hide the loss
in a growing, terrifying

art. Aging
we sit and spin, uncertain
that someone could love us,
seeing us.

IN THE PLANETARIUM

Man-made stars
speed across
a man-made space

and I lean back into the chair
as my mother must have
leaned back under the space
of my father's body.
A small light, a comet
approaches the sun.
My father's seed
approaches
my mother's. A soft laugh,
and I begin

to inhabit the space that grows
to hold me, cells divide,
moons break away
from planets, atoms spin

solar systems around me.
The comet's tail
is blown away from the sun.
My tail shrinks
in my mother's sea.
I grow fingers, toes. The arm
of the galaxy will hold me

when I leave one space
for another
space.

Horace Coleman

POEM FOR A "DIVORCED" DAUGHTER

if some nosey body asks "well,
is you got a daddy?"
give them the look that
writes "fool" on their face

if that aint enough & they
got to say "where he at?"
tell em "where he be!"

& if they *so* simple they
haven't got it yet
& try to stay in your business
to the degree of "well,
if he love you then how
come he aint here?"
you just sigh

poke your lip out low
ball your hands up
on your hips and let it slip:
"he loves me where he *is*"
    cause I do
    where I am

Philip Dacey

EDWARD WESTON
IN MEXICO CITY

Clouds, torsos, shells, peppers, trees, rocks, smokestacks.
Let neither light nor shadow impose on these things
To give them a spurious brilliance or romance,
Let the mystery be the thing itself revealed
There for us to see better than we knew we could.
The pepper. The simple green pepper. Not so simple.
There are no two alike. Sonya brings me new peppers
Every day and each one leads me to the absolute
In its own way. My friends tell me the peppers
I've done cause physical pain and make
Beads of sweat pop out on the forehead. Orozco,
As soon as he saw them, said they were erotic.
I know nothing of that. I only know
Or seek to know the inner reality
Of each particular fruit, the secret
It tries but fails to hide because
In truth it would be known and taken;
The secret is of itself and beyond itself.
This pepper here: follow its form
And you enter an abstract world,
Yet always what you are making love to
Is pepper, pepper, pepper. It can both be
And not be itself.

The naked female body
When looked at in the right, that is the askew, way
Can also disappear while remaining fully
Present. Yesterday Tina was lying naked on the azotea
Taking a sun-bath. I was photographing clouds.
Then I noticed her and came down to earth
To shoot three dozen negatives in twenty minutes.
It was Tina I took, yet, in this picture,
Her right hip rises to become a slope
On the other side of Nature, and the ribs
The ribs are hesitancies, a fineness that will go
Only so far amidst the mass then wait
To be discovered by the quiet ones.
Tina, hello and goodbye, and hello.

Just don't ask me to make a formula of this.
With a formula I'd catch only the appearance
Of a secret. But I must disappoint my friends
By always starting over again, day after day,
So that they say, "That's not a Weston, take it out!"
When the sun rises, I become ignorant again,
Unburdened of yesterday's victories. Today
It has been shells. Two shells, one a
Chambered Nautilus. I balanced them together,
One inside the other. White background, black background.
I even tried my rubber raincoat for a ground.
The shells would slip near to breaking.
I am near to breaking, too. That is my formula.
No, I break. I lose myself in the shells.
My friends are right, it's not a Weston, I'm gone,
Thank God. Gone into the luminous coils.
A coil's urge is to become a circle;
I'm what the coil needs to close the gap.
Pepper, torso, shell: they're circle, circle, circle.

And now for sleep. I'm going to look at the dark.
When I wake up, I won't know what I've seen
But I'll have seen it nevertheless. Tomorrow
I'll look at what's under the sun; if I see right,
I'll be remembering what I see tonight.

THE WAY IT HAPPENS

So you trust like the birds
in God's goodness.
You refuse to calculate.
You go naked.
This lasts years.
You wander.
You are never satisfied,
that is the point.
Again you renew your trust.
Soon you begin
to peck at the ground.
You do not notice this.
You only know
you savor small grain.
Then you learn to make
a new sound.
This gives you pleasure.
You think nothing of it.
Next you develop nubs
at your side that grow
and feather.
You use these
to tuck in your head.
You believe this is not strange.
Finally, for no good reason,
you beat them.
You begin to fly.
By now you are not thinking
at all
of what you are doing.

Melvin Dixon

RICHARD, RICHARD: *American Fuel*

"We both shuddered at the sound of Wright's burning body, quite audible in the still columbarium."

A witness

This far from Chicago and Natchez, Mississippi
air is tight with the sound of difficult vowels
in *"adieu," "j'arrive,"* or *rue de la Liberté.*

November 8, 1960, away for thirteen years,
you speak at the American Church, musing
over changes since journal entry of 1947:

"August 24: I have to remind myself
that I'm a Negro when I live in Paris.
There are whole days when I forget it.
France is, above all, a land of refuge."

Twenty days later you lie in intensive
care. The ghost of a woman
visits the night nurse in Neuilly.

Whose last fingers test your brow for heat?
Whose girlish laughter ropes about your neck?

Then December. Cimetière Père Lachaise.
Friends gather with family. Smoke
squeals up from furnace to chimney.
Some shudder at the noisy mixture
of cremation and cold weather.

But consider this: It is the chuckle
of Mary Dalton's sweet revenge,
the weighty echoes of Bessie's moan.

TOUR GUIDE: *La Maison des Esclaves*

He speaks of voyages:
men traveling spoon-fashion,
women dying in afterbirth,
babies clinging
to salt-dried nipples.
For what his old eyes still see
his lips have few words. Where
his flat thick feet still walk
his hands crack
into a hundred lifelines.

Here waves rush to shore
breaking news that we return
to empty rooms
where the sea is nothing calm.
And sun, tasting the skin
of black men,
leaves teeth marks.

The rooms are empty until he speaks.
His gutteral French is a hawking trader.
His quick Woloff a restless warrior.
His slow, impeccable syllables
a gentleman trader. He tells
in their own language
what they have done.

Our touring maps and cameras ready
we stand in the weighing room
where chained men paraded firm backs,
their women open, full breasts
and children
rows of shiny teeth.

Others watched from the balcony,
set the price in guilders, francs,
pesetas and English pounds. Later,
when he has finished we too
can leave our coins
where stiff legs dragged
in endless bargain.

He shows how some sat knee-bent
in the first room.
Young virgins waited in the second.
In the third, already red,
the sick and dying
gathered near the exit to the sea.

In the weighing room again
he takes a chain to show us
how it's done. We take
photographs to remember,
others leave coins to forget.
No one speaks
except iron on stone
and the sea
where nothing's safe.

He smiles for he has spoken
of the ancestors: his, ours.
We leave quietly, each alone,
knowing that they who come after us
and breaking
in these tides will find
red empty rooms
to measure long journeys.

                              with Sandra and Peggy,
                              Ile de Gorée, Senegal

MAN HOLDING BOY

Hunched forward under rain
like liquid steel upon his skin
he pushes ahead. The boy
locked to his chest, asleep.

He weighs this storm. His eyes
no longer begging clouds for comfort,
but testing the ground and the boy
still safe at his shoulders.

Rain spikes beating the old head
silence
once the boy awakes.
There are no more songs but his stirring.

After a photograph by John White

Franz Douskey

REGRESSING

I'm regressing
and can't read anything heavy

I have to let the books fall
and pick up something I can handle
like *House At Pooh Corner*

life has been good lately
nobody leaving no arguments
and the right amount of scarcity

today while walking through the park
I picked up wood to burn
and tonight the fire was lovely

the woman who lives inside me
sang English ballads and played recorder

now it's after midnight
and she's sleeping

right after I finish "Rabbit's Busy Day"
I'm going to turn off the light
curl against her
and forget I ever had ambition

Stephen Dunn

BEACHED WHALES OFF MARGATE

One day they just started rolling up,
six pilot whales from way out.
Two hundred people pushed three of them back, oh
it took hours. I tell you all this
because two hundred people usually hurt
what they touch. But not this time.
After it was done, they all stood around
for a while, like the humans they used to be,

lamenting the three who were dead.
Separateness set in slowly; an aerial shot
would have shown a group moving away
from its center, leaving in ones and twos
toward their large, inconsiderate houses.

FABLE OF THE WATER MERCHANTS

One day the water merchants came
to town, saying "Let the water pass
over our hands, it will taste better."
And the people agreed and became addicted
                    to that taste.
Then the water merchants threatened
to take away their hands, and the people
brought seed and chickens and placed them
                    at their feet.
But already the water merchants had carved
replicas of their hands out of wood
and secured them to the river bank.
                    The people said
"The water tastes different now"
and the water merchants replied "What you
are tasting, friends, is progress,"
and the people began to love it
and gave the merchants everything they wanted.

W. D. Ehrhart

TO MAYNARD ON THE LONG ROAD HOME

Biking at night with no lights
and no helmet, you were struck
and hurled sixty feet,
dead on impact.
The newspapers noted the irony:
surviving the war
to die like that, alone
on a hometown street.
I knew better.

Years before, on Christmas Day,
I met you on a road near Quang Tri;
a chance reunion of Perkasie boys
grown up together in a town
that feared God and raised sons
willing to die for their country.
"Who're you with?
Have you seen much action?
What the hell's going on here?"
All afternoon we remembered
our shared youth: the old boat
with Jeffy and the slow leak,
skipping Sunday school to read comics
and drink orange soda at Flexer's,
the covered bridge near Bryan's farm.
Though neither of us
spoke of it, we knew then
we had lost
more than our youth.

I show my poems to friends now and then,
hoping one or two might see
my idealistic bombast
in a new light;
the sharp turns of mood, anger
defying visible foundation,
inexplicable sadness.
How often they wonder aloud
how I managed to survive—
they always assume the war is over,
not daring to imagine our wounds,
or theirs, if it is not.
I think of you,
and wonder if either of us
will ever come home.

Harley Elliott

NUMBERS

The sky turns
an illuminated grey
this afternoon
behind each window of the house

suspended like an amulet

and I am waiting in my kitchen
drinking tea
waiting for the latest
news.

Among other things today
hope was officially forbidden
  78 miners
nine hundred feet down.

  It is easy to feel
the necessary sorrow

this formal tragedy of ciphers
    coming as it does
    at 5 o'clock
from a white cube of abstractions

        the radio
    placed casually
crossways on the refrigerator.

        Later commentators
    will assure me
it was a day like all days.
I will have had another
cup of pale tea
drifting between what is common
in the black jeweled earth
        of west virginia
 and this grey sky

        And at other times
I may stop
trying to understand the words
for a number of men
a number of feet deep
    isolated as this
    afternoon echo
    of water falling in a sink

as the radio begins knowingly
        dealing in numbers.

LANDSCAPE WORKERS

Down on the riverbank
the men were pulling roses

no matter what the heat
they still seemed
close to winter

    and primitive
about the heavy owls that rose
and fell invisible
for long and fearful moments.

    It was easy then
to think of them as brutes
or bent men   living it all
out on the lips of rivers

    except seen when
they stood with evening wages
        arms of soft
uprooted roses
at five o'clock

like myths
awaiting an occasion.

John Engman

RAINER MARIA RILKE RETURNS FROM THE DEAD TO ADDRESS THE JUNIOR MILITARY SCHOOL AT SANKT PÖLTEN

Boys, these aches and pains will make us men.
It all depends on how you hurt yourself. Once,
I read about a boy my age, in *Time,* who became rain
by stepping on stones that explode beneath human weight.
Defying gravity, he rained from earth into the air and then
he rained more naturally as red and yellow ashes from the trees.
Boys, it all depends on how you hurt yourself. We will be shot.
In uniform. Again and again. In France or Spain. But in uniform
boys are men: when I was small my mother dressed me in a bonnet
and yellow frock. And I admit my admiration for the muscles of
                                                             Rodin.
Sometimes love has been mistaken for the way we use our hands
but don't let them call you women. Let bedsprings scream: *Enough!*
I am a man. I saw Prague divided by a falling leaf.
And from a clinic window at Valmont I saw red and yellow leaves
falling and being blown away—that taught me all I want to know
about delayed allegiances. What makes us men will kill us all.
We stay alive by dreaming of the boys we used to be, who'd never
recognize us now: priests and aviators dressed in black or gray,
who don't know what to make of what, who tremble and obey.

Sandra Maria Esteves

FROM THE COMMONWEALTH

So you want me to be your mistress
and find dignity in a closed room
because you say your first real love is music
even though I too am music
the sum total of contrary chords and dissonant notes
occasionally surviving in mutilated harmony
even though I could fill you so full
to grow outside yourself
and walk with you thru opalescent gardens

But you only want me to be your Sunday afternoon mistress
and I have to recycle this flow of ebony tailored ambition
limit the mother in me that wants to intoxicate herself
in the center of your soul
not watch alien wives trade you off for multi colored trinkets
flashing against the real you

Understanding what a whore sophistication really is
I reject a service role
a position I've truly hated whenever it was forced upon me

And it's true that I am a drifter, a wanderer
a gypsy whose objective in life is to travel in whole circles
that resemble the path of Venus around the Sun

I never reveled in washing clothes
or reached orgasms from dirty dishes
but I didn't mind being part of someone
who could help me to be me
with all my transient contradictions

And I am a woman, not a mistress or a whore
or some anonymous cunt whose initials barely left an inpression
on the foreskin of your nationhood

Y si la patria es una mujer
then I am also a rebel and a lover of free people
and will continue looking for friction in empty spaces
which is the only music I know how to play.

VANGUARDIA

they walk on the edge of the world
wage a war of peace
feed fires of creation
write the book of reality
nourish it
direct the wind of nations
disect the hate monger
pull apart the tentacles
with a prick of blood and intention
slowly building a fortress
soul upon soul
cement of sweat
sleepless dreamers
daggers of birth
they come in waves
of songs in pain
in fields of strengths
and growing stalks of thunder
they come from wet wombs
totally pushing the walls
of empty existence
breaking the fabric and crust
of rotting by-products

they come with faithful love
yearning to touch a deepless place
seeking a point of truth
that loves the universe
and sheds tears of joy
for the dawn that only rises
in the heart of unity.

Alice Fulton

HOW TO SWING THOSE OBBLIGATOS AROUND

He had shag hair and a boutique.
In the bar he told me I had too much class
to be a telephone operator and I told him
he should have been thirty in 1940:
a gangster with patent leather shoes
to shine under girls' skirts & a mother
who called him sonny.   He should have
crashed a club where they catered
to the smart set, disposing of
the bouncer with   you spent three months
in a plaster cast the last time
you tangled with me   and I should have been
the singer in tight champagne
skin waiting for him to growl
I don't know how to begin
this beguine but you certainly know how to
swing those obbligatos around   and we
would fox-trot till a guy
he knew from Sing-Sing cut in.
And he said he loved old flicks
I should come up to his place & see
the art deco ashtrays on his shag rug
that I shouldn't waste myself
at bell tel but marry him
and take his business calls and
I said   how many years do you get
if they give you life.

CHAIN LETTERS

Dear Lady,
you have been selected.
Simply follow these procedures:
Consider yourself
a franchised venture, a motel.
Appearances matter, after all
there are other motels—
some with picnic grounds!
Novelty cannot be over emphasized—
be creative! Consider developing
your appendix into a third breast.

When the exterior is sandblasted
bright, begin public relations.
Harness your voice
to the wild trolley of enthusiasm.
Oil your neck
till the head nods only North and South.
Practice manual dexterity,
for in music, you are a born percussionist.
Train your ear to the rhythm
of applause, the hidden muscle it needs.

Make sure your vacancy sign is well-lit.

In one month sixty men will fall
headlong into your hungry rooms.
You can ingest them with this season's lips.
Women who kept this chain intact
attest to its success: Cleopatra,
Scarlett, Marilyn, and your mother.
Break the chain
and the world's stray cats
will seek your narrow door;
African violets, Haviland,
your only collectibles.

Copy this ten times and pass it on.

Roger Gaess

VIEWING RUSSIAN PEASANTS
FROM A LENINGRAD-BOUND TRAIN

During the night
perhaps
they had painted the greens
peasant green. Only now unveiled
by the sun, with an artist's pride
and the sureness of a magician;
its arms whispering through the birches
as the page of early morning
unrolls its fresh red carpet
red as the hint of the apple's ripeness
red as the cheek of a healthy child
or the revolution's blood.

On long shadows
the distant peasants move.
I see their pitchforks aflame
with the light of a new day,
want to walk among them: the wind
blowing back the wheat,
blowing strong against our faces.

FALL LIGHTLY ON ME

In its own way rising to crest by me, the day
tempts restless dawnlight and the furtive gilt shadows,
edges the gauze of mist here for its ends,
enters here at Autumn's near edge, as trees

unlock themselves like prisoners, victims
of choice's seasoned fruit: dream, or
dream of dream: corn-mother now in flight
across the fields, brow of the earth
with darkening furrows, wild feet
in the nightlight; wild ways
in the lightnight, corn-spirit, wreath
of the finest ears
on the head of that prettiest girl, maple-yellow
tresses and woodbine breasts, skin of
white, white-light skin, wandering
past the memory of the garden, beyond
the recall of the ripeness of the Fall, wandering
while limbs near naked leave the earth,
to enter my room of softness and walls
and, like the rain, to fall,
fall lightly on me
as if remembering the way to Spring.

Tess Gallagher

BLACK MONEY

His lungs heaving all day in a sulphur mist,
then dusk, the lunch pail torn from him
before he reaches the house, his children
a cloud of swallows about him.
At the stove in the tumbled rooms, the wife,
her back the wall he fights most, and she
with no weapon but silence
and to keep him from the bed.

In their sleep the mill hums and turns
at the edge of water. Blue smoke
swells the night and they drift
from the graves they have made for each other,
float out from the open-mouthed sleep
of their children, past banks and businesses,
the used car lots, liquor store, the swings in the park.

The mill burns on, now a burst of cinders,
now whistles screaming down the bay, saws jagged
in half light. Then like a whip
the sun across the bed, windows high with mountains
and the sleepers fallen to pillows
as gulls fall, tilting
against their shadows on the log booms.
Again the trucks shudder the wood framed houses
passing to the mill. My father
snorts, splashes in the bathroom,
throws open our doors to cowboy music
on the radio, hearts are cheating,
somebody is alone, there's blood in Tulsa.
Out the back yard the night-shift men rattle
the gravel in the alley going home.
My father fits goggles to his head.

From his pocket he takes anything metal,
the pearl-handled jack knife, a ring of keys,
and for us, black money shoveled
from the sulphur pyramids heaped in the distance
like yellow gold. Coffee bottle tucked in his armpit
he swaggers past the chicken coop,
a pack of cards at his breast.
In a fan of light beyond him
the Kino Maru pulls out for Seattle,
some black star climbing
the deep globe of his eye.

A SHORT HISTORY OF THE BETTER LIFE

What we were doing then was making good company
out of too-bad-next-time sweet-contentment-guys
and other busy and in business men, busy
away from home so the children kept us and we
were in the home and later out of it so to say
"Not us" and "Not them" and "Not me" until we
were busy as if doing what a boss wanted, what
the man-boss wanted was going to buy us the extra
we had got used to needing in the busy ways
of wanting the next thing
more than you could
have. We got to be the best company we had
with our children in the nurseries and our men
in airports and car pools and ourselves
tooting around in the second car
to the some-fun job for the just barely-pay,
stimulating our interest in the outside world
where even more was going on
without us, running our part-time with no
benefits into overtime with no time
for anybody but ourselves doing it
for too-little-not-enough-somebody. Which gets
you into poetry
which is language enough for saying
what's been said until it's heard as music,
usable as music that two-steps
into your home-town of a heart and tells you
this is not a Marxist poem to be used up like a
grocery list for the better life you
should have had back there in
somebody else's young-time-good-looks. No sir. No
maam. For this is Yes Station and we all
got to get out here, got to get out
of the music.

WHEN YOU SPEAK TO ME

Take care when you speak to me.
I might listen, I might
draw near as the flame
breathing with the log, breathing
with the tree it has not
forgotten. I might
put my face
next to
your face
in your nameless trouble,
in your trouble
and name.

It is a thing I learned
without learning; a hand
is a stronger mouth, a kiss could
crack the skull, these
words, small steps
in the air calling
the secret hands, the mouths
hidden in the flesh.

This isn't robbery.
This isn't your blood for my
tears, no confidence
in trade or barter. I may
say nothing back
which is to hear
after you the fever
inside the words we say
apart, the words we say so hard
they fall apart.

HARMLESS STREETS

Many times a last time I will look
into this room like walking
fully clothed into a floodstream.
Under the candelabra in a hotel lobby or
on the train where the commuters ruffle
their papers, or standing in a corridor of
elevators, it will come before me
as though I could never leave.

When I came to you
like a woman who dressed herself in the morning,
who spread the fan of her hair
at night on your pillow, they were with us already,
those days we would live
out of what you had done alone.

You were the man of fear and omens
who cast his own death in the slant of a tree or
looking up, caused a star inside the head
to break from space, but more often
it was loss of the simplest talisman, expected,
a slight regret that could end all.

Mostly no one saw what was done. The dead
were unspectacular, scattered and inarticulate,
preferring to be handled and stepped over,
though at times they seemed to argue
among themselves, a continual racket about the beauty
of the universe or the piteousness of the human
voice, filling the ancient night
with their elaborate nostalgia.

Once there was no doubt. That one
was yours and you walked to him where he lay
and you took from his pockets
a picture, no wife or child, but an image of
himself. If he had raised up on one arm
and said in the language of the dying, 'Take this.

Remember me,' you would not have done less.
But no, the dead have no such rights and the living
are merciless, saying, 'Lie down. Be counted.'

Each day his eyes are opened on your wall
among the emblems that returned whole legions, no glad
survivors, but hostage to these harmless streets.
And I who did not see what was done
have seen him cut off at the neck, have heard him speak
full bodied. He is offended
there on your wall in his one death, in your one life.
He has changed his mind
and wants only to be forgotten, not entirely, no
just enough to surprise your continuing
pain. Pain that continues is not pain, outleaps

the body. That soldier
in the poster near the armchair
keeps running toward us extending his wing
of blood. It is too red. It is only the color
red. I have tried
to see it otherwise, but cannot.

You are right. What can I know, a woman
who was never there? Empathy, sad apron, I take you
on and off. In loving
it was the same. I almost
felt. Your pleasure was almost mine.

The white tree near the window
looks in on your bed, the flowered sheets
where I drift with the parachutes of the men
falling like delicate organs into watery fields.
But what can I know? I
who may not be counted, womb
of your secret shame and silences:
companion, mourner, thief.

Brendan Galvin

GLASS

What the warbler must have seen
was the world swung round;
without turning back
she was flying into
a distance already passed through:

another side of the woodpile
she had just cleared in a single pitch,
and beyond, through the middle ground
of pines, the background glitter
of running sea she had skipped above
like a flat stone thrown so well
it touches down on water
all the way to the other shore.

Swung round,
only slightly blurred.
Trees twinning,
far water grained,
air of a density . . .

then that split-second insight

into splashes of newspaper
and clothing,
filtered through
final dusts of light.

As perhaps,
in our last seconds,
we are swung round
to live ourselves back through
each particular,

to fall faster and faster
out of loves, out of
changes of clothes,

whole snows lifting skyward
becoming autumn leaves lifting
back into green trees,
the dead stepping out of
crumbling loam,

at the last, seed and egg
unraveling, falling away.

And all
in the time
it takes a flat stone to skip over water
and be let in.

A PHOTO OF MINERS

USA, 1908

With trees backing them
instead of the pit's mouth,
they could have been
at a fifth-grade picnic.
But the spitballer won't grow into
his father's jacket, and a ladder
of safety pins climbs the front of
the class clown. Stretch,
who got tall the soonest,
has the air of a chimney sweep,
and here is a little grandfather
in brogans and rag gloves,
his face shoved between two shoulders
his arms are draping,
his eyes flashing the riding lights
of pain. They are a year's

supply, average age, give or take
a year: ten. Don't look for
a bare foot at a devil-may-care
angle on one of the rails,
or a habitable face for a life
you might have led—that
mouth is rigid as a mail slot,
the light on those hands predicts
common graves. Does anything transcend
the walleyed patience of beasts,
the artless smirk on the boy
with the high forehead
who thinks he will croon his way
out of this?

Marilyn Hacker

ORDINARY WOMEN   I

I am the woman you see in Blooming-
dale's ruffling the rack of children's sweaters
on sale, trying on tweed slacks in Better
Sportswear, which I won't buy, browsing and homing
in on unmatched striped sheets on January
Clearance. Rapt with textures, women escalate
leisurely. This is our protectorate.
Our brown or pink skins flush over furry
or frayed coats in smoothing taupe light. We do
not shuffle aside for the man, who is
not here, who built this shelter, our consuming
career. What I am saying to you is
I am the woman you will see blooming
up from our terror, with women: me, you.

ORDINARY WOMEN   II

For June Jordan and Sara Miles

Mrs. Velez of the Tenants' Association
zig-zags her top-heavy shopping cart through
the usual palette of dogshit, brick-red
to black on grimy leftover snow.
Tenement roofs' stone scrollwork
soot-chiaroscuro on the almost-equinoctial
sky. Old Mrs. Cohen, who still wears a marriage-wig,
stiff-legs the stoop with Food City-bagged garbage.
Slashed bags everywhere spill chicken-bones,
orange peels, crushed milk cartons, piss-soaked
Pampers, broken toys.
Sweat-cracked loafers, runover orange work-shoes, silver-painted
platform shoes, running-stripe sneakers, a cast on one foot
and newspaper-stuffed single shoe, electric-blue-patent-leather-
style-fake-yellow-snakeskin-trim-shoes, stand,
pace,
shuffle,
Bop a little,
in front of the liquor store; the hands man brown-bagged Ripple.
She has a daughter named Tequila,
little and Black and wiry and so is she,
her name's Joanne.
Yellow-trousered Tequila, rising three,
dashes from the separator to the laundry scales,
past two broken dryers.
Sometimes she plays with Iva on the slide.
"I'm OK, I'm goin' to night school, studying
bookkeeping,
but I gotta leave Tequila with my brother—
that's him."
He must be nine,
little and Black and wiry, leafs
SPIDERMAN, THE INCREDIBLE HULK beside him
on the bracketed row of plastic chairs.
Tequila's run outside.
"Joseph, go *get* her!" He does.

Joanne has a textbook, *American History,*
all-sized thumb-smudges on the library
binding. She has me write my name and number
on a creased notebook-leaf shoved inside.
"What you doin' Tequila? Stay by me, you hear!"
I feel my old brown sheepskin's London label,
my red wool ERA cap . . . Joseph herds
Tequila towards the thrumming washing-
machines. She
scooters a canvas basket to the porthole.
Her left blue Flintstones sneaker is untied.
Tile walls sweat steam and soap. Compact Anne Desirée,
the proprietaire, has my laundry folded
into the Macy's shopping-bag. "Comment ça va?"
"Très bien, merci." "Et ta fille?" "Grandissante,
à l'école au moment. Merci bien, au revoir. Bye,
Joanne, Joseph, Tequila!"
Threadbare brown corduroy coat, Army Surplus safari jacket,
orphaned suit-coat, raddled blue anorak, black leather bomber
jacket, pastel polyester plaid with calf-length back-split skirts
elbow outside the liquor store;
the hands man brown-bagged Ripple.
The woman who stands on street-corners stands
on the street-corner, her coffee-bean
skin ashy, her plump face Thorazine
swollen. Thin grey coat gaps open
on short white housedress gapped open
on bolstered brown knock knees.
Fragile flesh puffs sink her huge wet eyes,
not looking across the street, or down the street,
not looking at the sidewalk or the sky.

Lawson Fusao Inada

THE DISCOVERY OF TRADITION
For Toshio Mori and John Okada

I can tell you about this, sure enough,
and I'll do the best job I can
out here in the perimeters,
but you've got to do it for your self.

And I had been told and told about it,
studied it, even, square in the face
and gone away wanting from home.
I had to feel it to really know.

What do you do in a case like that?
You don't even know what's missing
and the first thing you've got to do
is know what it is you need to know . . .

I. The Work in Progress

It was winter (gestures, wind, breathing),
things needed tending (men in a forest, armloads of wood)
and, of course, I needed tending too (a dropped log rolling down
the slope).

After all, was I to simply
see my self through again,
repeating what had been done
as its own accomplishment?

What would I see when I looked back,
emerging into spring and the echoes of children
calling to me their questions in the lower meadow?

After all, the descent to the valley
is deceptively easy, and therein lies the task:
to hold your own
is the most beautiful and natural thing—
a hand full of this, a hand full of that—
but the rest of the world comes
summoned at the asking,
implicit in the invitation of your just being here,
and before you know it
children have arrived with visitors and leaves with the faces of fish
and before you know it,
high on the slopes, once more as usual, it starts to snow.

II. The Progress in Work

(Look: a car moving down a road
            banked with snow,
            the tires thick with traction
            grabbing and crunching.)

(Look: a classroom full of flowers,
            sunlight full of books
            and everyone laughing.)

Ah, yes. And still, though,
it had come easy
because I didn't know any better.

I want to know what I'm doing,
to emerge, to learn, to keep going.

How has it been with you?

III. The Observance of Rituals

Toppling, an eclipse off the top of my head now, up there
where the ranges run, the smooth things moving with the wind itself
as it counts, decked out in crevices that matter and laughing
with the whole thing in particular, part and parcel of the what what are
when the mind is full,

when the life is full,
when there is nothing missing in the eye and senses rocking
back and forth in the continuum
humming with stars, the light winding down and starting up again
to concern us all—

    what crosses me crosses you with the force of shadows of sound
    emerging and merging into where things quicken and everything
    is enough—

rippling, the vision at the bottom of the self, here, down
here as we bob and walk in the moment of momentum and the drop
                                     off coming
who knows where which is why we keep going into it with the force of
                                       fortune
we know is there giving back and going forth rippling and toppling,

rippling and toppling as we go.

IV. The Emergence of Topics

It starts to rain. It starts to snow.
Whatever "it" is, it's going through some heavy combinations
up there in the mountains, mind you,
whole lot of shaking going on
including some occasional sunlight, thank you,
and just the whole bunch of stuff in general
and on down the ranks to us in burrows
tucking heads under wings
the sweet way we like to think
wet women will always do and did.

I'm sitting here with Toshio and John,
talking over such momentous things:

    "Long ago, children, I lived in a country called Japan. Your
    grandpa was already in California earning money for my boat
    ticket. The village people rarely went out of Japan and were
    shocked when they heard I was following your grandpa as soon
    as the money came."

                Toshio Mori, *Yokohama, California*

"Two weeks after his twenty-fifth birthday, Ichiro got off a bus at Second and Main in Seattle. He had been gone four years, two in camp and two in prison."

John Okada, *No-No Boy*

The rain, the snow, the steady stream.
The observance of rituals.
The tribute of tributaries.
The rain, the snow, the steady stream.

This is how it began, for me.

V. The Tribute of Tributaries

The book comes out of the wrist,
with fingers.
It is a pool, an ocean, a delta:

the whorls of words for dreaming in the evening,
the lines of streams to follow on the palm, meandering,
spaces to see through, to get to and around,
pages, fingers, forests, frames;

and all of this for holding and waving,
for carrying around.

And this one is Toshio.
And this one is John.

Where had they been before?
Here, here, is the only answer.
Here, as ever more.

Those older ones, those I had always known
receding into the distance with women,
holding me at arm's length
like uncles from mountains
gripping steering wheels and going by late
in trucks full of business,
sometimes handing me
tickets to a carnival, coins to a show.

Those older ones—
I had to claim them as my own.
I had to sit down with them
in a room ripe with rumor,
blatant with shadows
and claim them as my own.

And in the end, of course,
it was they who claimed me,
who bade me to be—
unafraid, unashamed—
who bade me to see,
clasping my face
with the faith of love.

"I am your mother's brother."
"I am your father's brother."

"Come."

VI. The Coming and The Going

We were on the shore that would not be denied.
The ocean filled the eye with the wetness of memory
as we were witness to the journey we would know,
the long journey across the tatami of water
away from those who lay sleeping and would go on.

We were on the shore that would not be denied.
It was our own shore, the strength we had known.
We took this with us through the rage and the roar.
We came, we came, to Washington, to California, to Oregon.

VII. The Going and The Coming

Toshio, being the oldest,
settled down.
He had had enough of travels and travail,
the hard times cropping up in rows,
and decided instead to learn the language
of plants and English.

The plants, naturally,
sprang from his hands
as a matter of course—
they did this all day long;
the English had to be pampered
under the tip of the tongue
but it, too, came furling from his fingers
firm and familiar in the rows of his own—
some nights, they surprised him with dawn.

So he worked hard, and the growing was glorious.
All around were horizons.
What he learned, he earned, and vice-versa.
And this allowed John to go to college.

And John was the bright light
come the blackout.
And this allowed us all to go to war.

And it was a strange war of wire
coming at us from all sides.
But Toshio kept writing.

And when the war was over,
John was standing there
in a uniform and a novel.

Sometimes, we would sit watching the world
march by the living room, gesturing and threatening;
but Toshio pointed out the frost on the wisteria
barbed with beauty in the softness of the light;
and John showed how the eyes of the hysterical
froze at the lashes, barbed and blurred.

I learned there, the power of the word.

VIII. The Power of The Word

And so, in the middle of winter,
        in the middle of mountains,
        in the middle of night,

in the middle of a room,
in the middle of my hands,
I found my way again.

And so, in the middle of my life,
    I found my way to you.

IX. The Meaning of Tradition

Put it this way: tradition is a means, a connection.

Put it this way: tradition is a vision, a core.

Put it this way: tradition is a lineage, a continuum.

Put it this way: tradition is a freedom, a whole.

X. The Freedom of Tradition

Lest it seem too dramatic or mystical, allow me to assure you that of what I speak is in reality very real—that is, it's a *feeling* I'm talking about, which is very natural and how we really live, which is very dramatic and mystical.

And what it's done for me is give me the feeling that I have so much more to give.

The feeling is skin, soul, bones, being together. And the beautiful thing is, you can even take it for granted.

Or you can think you live without it, as I did, but it's there all the time, like time, and all it takes is a single person to be it and recognize it.

Then, whatever you do will be in the tradition.

And so I say I work in the tradition of Toshio and John: welcome.

And though I know it is one of beauty and power and greatness, that does not really distinguish it; it is, and needs no justification: you've got your relatives and I've got mine. And we've got a multitude of mutual futures.

Besides, the names, the labels, can be restricting, misleading—and why confuse and exclude our selves?

Tradition is a source.

Tradition is a way.

Tradition is a place to start.

XI. The Sources of Tradition

(non-translations from
the Japanese-American)

1. The Spider and The Squid

These noises and faces and gestures we make,
we borrowed from the spider and the squid.

Notice the effect when we try to communicate:
we snare them closer or propel our selves away.

2. Lizards, Water, Wind

And as for calligraphy, lizards, water, wind—
among others, which is what we are—
make tracks in all their familiar patterns.

Their contribution is the traction of tradition:
each shape, each piece of punctuation
is a place to go and stay, to leap from—

and in this most graceful way do we carry on.

3. Dancing Creatures

It is no wonder poets speak of "feet."

4. The Novel of The Snail

No matter that it scrolls a mile long;
each line must always have its start:

from this observance we created margins.

5. The Tradition of The Sun

All writers wave their pages to the sun.

To wave back is the tradition of the sun.

XII. The Rhythm of Tradition

(water boiling) Well,
(voices outside) it's
(someone is launching a boat somewhere) about
(Just the other day, some of us folks
were making mochi in Henry's backyard, using the big
hollowed out hip and torso of an oak stump for a holder
and an ax handle stuck into half a baseball bat as the pounder) that
(and we, the hands, including Toshio and John,
looked up between the force of our strokes
and smiled, since mochi-making
brings your energy out into the rice and air
where it can be shared again) time
(and Henry, blowing thick mochi breath
into the thick mochi sky, said
"I wonder if we're the only ones in town doing this now.") again
(And I said "Maybe in the state, maybe in the nation,
maybe in the entire world because it's night over there and . . . "
And Henry said "So someone's making love."
And we all began to laugh
because mochi-making is also a continual process) to
(and is going on all the time:) say
(the rhythm of tradition.) goodbye.

D. L. Klauck

DIRTY JOKE

every sunday
in the state prison
convicts flock to church
strange as wasps
to flypaper
protestants first hour
catholics second

old man jackson attends both
knowing
what a wrong choice means

all he has in the world
is the crippled sparrow
found in the yard last fall

everyone mocks him
wing never healed right
dumb bird can't fly

but jackson
thanks two gods for that
every sunday

EINSTEIN'S FATHER

i tell him *eat your dinner*
he arranges it in unfamiliar patterns
assigns obscure names to common things
can't recall days or months or seasons

prepares for school during holidays
has no talent for game or contest
stares for hours at nothing i can see

somedays he ties his shoes together
wonders why he falls down stairs
always bumps into walls and furnishings
catches his hands in closing doors
wears boots and gloves to bathe in
has trouble finding his way back home
loses patience with prayer and tradition

while i've tried raising him to be normal
still he collects sunlight in a leaded box
speaks to dark worlds in awkward tongues
lord knows i've suffered for his mistakes
but i don't care what people might think
i'm just concerned for the boy's survival
i won't be around to protect him forever

on my lap before he could walk
i'd imagine him becoming a great man
albert i'd say *someday you'll be famous*
perhaps a composer or a skilled surgeon
everyone will hold you in highest esteem
your name as well known as goethe's
though even a mason's craft is honorable

the reasonable dream of any father
but now i'll gladly settle for a beggar
if he avoids becoming criminal
if the dull madman in him remains dull
this graceless mindless boy
who lacks the imagination to be cautious
lacks the ignorance to be afraid

MYTHS

in ancient china under rule of shang
shang priests fashioned bones of virgins
into delicate but lethal weapons

myths of power ascribed to such weapons
made the bodies of lovely young girls
marketable

crops of sacred daughters were raised
believing *love is the most disgraceful sin*

terrorized by throbbing libidos
violation of chastity was rare
offenders suffered dishonor
in public execution while
the privileged chaste were honored
in ritual sacrifice

proud parents adorned
with jewels and silks—
costumes of a dignity assumed unblemished
by a daughter's sanctity

homely sisters forced
to labor fields
attend the chosen as maid-servants
and mate with dreadful old men

virile male youths segregated
to lives of military celibacy
protecting mythologies
with bone weaponry

this is how it is with the awful
exaggerations of power:

dynasties founded on bones of children
dragons in the forms of men

there are no angels
the earth herself a boneless victim
and justice
the most corruptible metaphor
of a faltered humanity

Lyn Lifshin

MARTHA GRAHAM

you have so little
time she says each
instant is so

exciting   at
first in the early
days i was made
fun of   i was
in my long

underwear   i
took off my
bangles   we
took women
off toe shoes
i wanted life
the way it
is

long neck her
lips like
a young girl's

only dance if you
have to i
said if you
think you might
want a family
a home   don't

her hair pulled
back her face
wide open

MARRAKESH WOMEN

pulled from their fathers
at night under dark veils

to a house where they'll
never stop working

Weaving   making
babies   till the husband

takes another wife
Laughter is rare

the women crouch
before the huge looms

unfold gardens   the
deepest red   rivers

flowing thru light
and shadow   a scene

described by their
mothers   they

bury all things   their
love and fear in the

red   forget the baby
in the hammock   the world

they are cut off
from as cut off as the

dark blood strands of wool

REMEMBER THE LADIES

rachelle weeping   painting 1772

some mothers lived to
bury all their children

charles peale   his baby
dying of small pox
painted the child
quiet as stone
her arms tied with
a satin ribbon
at her side

lace covered pillow
the sheets over the
bottom of her legs
like a little orange
on a pillow

years later he painted
the mother in tears
touching her own skin

resting at the
edge of the bed

like it was a
table she was
studying her home
work on

the picture hung years
in the painter's house
covered by a curtain

with the sign "Before you
draw this curtain consider
whether you will
offend a mother or father
who has lost a child"

Lou Lipsitz

BROOKLYN SUMMER

For the Friedlands

She cooked all day
her skin turning rosy
and the walls of the house
seeming to sweat
like heavy leaves in the jungle.

She had a chicken in the oven
even though it was summer
and the open windows
only brought news
of boiling children
falling in the street.

Then, at the end,
she wiped her face,
thoughtlessly,
like a swimmer
stepping out of the ocean.

And the father came home
and washed
and my friend Gerry
came in
and then they enjoyed everything,
sitting for an hour
sweating and talking
at the table
like guerillas who have won the war.

And then, for the
first time in years,
she went out
on the fire escape with them,
and I heard her laugh
when someone blew smoke rings,
and she slept with her foot
hanging over the edge
like a root.

THE PIPES

You will not be like those who turn their faces away
when death moves toward them like an ocean.

You will know him. You will look at him,
slowly, opening your mind little by little,
just as you sat as a child with the water rolling
around your legs; staring until the ocean became known to you.
And you will go back often, carrying away with you
the strange moisture of that sea
and a desire to be luminous and unarmed.

I think of the Indians of the Columbian jungle,
and their pipes of gay colors.
They will dig clay for the pipes
in one spot only,
on the territory of their enemies—
a valley guarded by traps and poisoned arrows.
They say only those pipes are real.

AFTER VISITING A HOME FOR DISTURBED CHILDREN

Broken lamps!
Their faces shine with a destroyed light:
Illumination
of tangled gestures, of silent beatings,
of the black river of childhood.
Terrible light.

A light to which I cannot speak.
Light of corroding marriages.
Light of secret cries lost
like the signals of minute stars.
Light of empty basements
in which children have carefully hidden their names.

At night, unable to sleep,
I stare out the window at the empty road
and bits of light shine out of the dark,
intense, searching,
like the eyes of a girl who is buried alive.

THE SIRENS

even the sirens
got tired
weary of
always calling
whoever it was to
come closer
with
their unavoidable
song

for a while
their arms ached
and their
voices struggled
in their throats
but then they
found other things
—a way of
talking among
themselves as they
collected rocks on the beach;
and they slowly learned
to carve
and to tie fish
nets delicate as
the webs of spiders.

Charles Lynch

JAM FA JAMAICA

munch lime   sip sky juice   slurp kiskimo pine
honey bee bus   from mo bay   tree behine   chat?flat?scratch?
climb eel el spine bluesy mt. revery
twelfth tribe gullies airwaves upon babylon
quick step   wait-a-bit   smell english mon
me no sen   you no come   cockpit country   is a halt
whence lamb's blood benevolence   visions from judah
hazard apocalyptic name   mane rye-chee-ous-ness
driven off plains   sieve plots   hand idle land idle
abeng call pall: *garoo garoo garoooooo*

shrink credit   crime caution   daily   gleaning
surfeit shoal   dovecote whistling   toady motto
cricket creak out of anyone people won people

runaway bay bay   stout dragon's creeping fish redeemer
tout lout flagon   fume barreling rheum

grueled effigy keen exhorbitant gas
impossible to purchase face cream masque
clean house!   after maid!   all   the life

me whan go home   heart down   head turn   a round
bout trench town six bends yard boil

hewer of wood   drawer of water   caster of stone
smile gem acre   hope's gardener   marooned coral aisle
in heart land garvey nanny nyam bammy   rule mon-a-cool

star ward   herons dip   poise   sleek viney web
ibo eye   feeshire   cool tumbling spring
wheel on   clipped prophecy   cane hack   tough black scar line
tug push pull bump sway drift raft

captain mento lean streaks mauve sunset:
"ahm troo mahn   budt ama pooer mahn yusee
ah hav likkle skoolin   ah hav to wok verry verry odddd
budt pooer mahn dai soon come   so-shall-eesm bettah fa awl"

back pasture   salt gut   spur tree
rat trap   lambs river   ginger hill
oracabessa   rio bueno

salvation army blares liberty
in twilight square of port antonio

SIMFUNNY OF THEE HOLD WHORL

lancing   enhancing
attend end th'air leash
beach due in one dimension: blooey

imagine   slaves prancing
raffia   strand   crossed wind

wards off ration passion
chancing foam   felt
glancing elmina quay

iron anklets   duncing   deprave
slaves they culled it
three in D   mention it   blue

rave   grave   slaveslaveslaveslavesla
at bend of their leech
behave   bleat   won dimension   blu-eeee!!!

imagine   slave prance
rough   ya stranded   cross   winded

cave in   ration passion
gray atlantis   weep elmina quay

quaint turn of phrase
dancin the slaves
enticer than
square
dancin   nicer
than slaughtrin the slaves
choosin the slaves
wattrin the slaves
quattrin the slaves
losin the slaves

dancing the slaves was what they called it
slaves danced to dispel fixed melancholy

oar blues   demon shun

Cleopatra Mathis

CELEBRATING THE MASS OF CHRISTIAN BURIAL
For Anna Barry, 1883-1977

The air changes, blooms.
The geranium in your room across the yard
is blank as the chair. March has come—
the clouds swell and break, lifting the sky
out of gray. Last month you promised
this clearness loosening the dogwood.

I can see past your house and mine,
past the road that borders
the canal, a child of the river. Water collides,
creates reflection. I recognize

a different landscape, the detail of black
and red lace on the river, the small sun
through the trees.

This kind of sight is transient,
I know it won't be the same again.
Three days ago you held a clear glass
of sherry and willed a change.
The removal of ourselves is like this,
the quick fog of our lives
rising past the boundaries we know, past the season
of our own deaths.

Judith McCombs

PACKING IN WITH A MAN

I had thought I would need him
                              love under stars
my fellow explorer
                    Packing into the badlands
following the earth
                    my needs were quite different

Where the hollows of foothills
                              opened their silence
he kept asking questions
                         Where the shoulders of cliffs
trusted our shadows
                    he plotted with maps

Wherever we went
                    he needed escapes
to the road & the car
                    to the money he trusted

When the nighthawk attacked
                            he timed its return
When the bright quartz signalled
                                    he broke it for samples
When the fire worm began
                            he drowned it with napalm
In the high arroyos
                    his bootprints trampled
the fingers of cedar
                    the prints of the bones

He refused to follow
                    cloud furrows, brain furrows,
the buried windings
                    of water & silt,
the dirt track remembered
                            in a dream of creatures

I couldn't believe
                    enough for us both
So I took what I needed
                            Less shelter, more fear

Ken McCullough

VOICES IN THE WINTER

I wake from my nightsweats to build up the fire.
The sun comes up on the sacred mountain,
there is snow on the stunned pines around Blue Lake.
As the dog next door begins his cockcrow barking
the dead man leaves off scratching at my window.
I've been dreaming about you here beside me
in a flimsy shift, and the scent of citrus
still mingles in the room with pinon smoke.

But there were voices floating in the vigas,
voices that woke me. I have been listening to the
radio too much this week. I heard the blue
lights glint on the President's blue mandibles
as he left the mike, satisfied, on his way
to dinner, and I know that as he walked, no
one with him saw his footprints fill with blood.
Kissinger, a man from some secret phylum,
an unctuous viola, allays our fears. A
nice touch— we believe a man with an accent.
Bamboo gates shriek open, our boys come home.

But then I hear the last shipment of corpses
filled with heroin ripen in their caskets
knowing I helped unload a planeful of those
shiny tins eight summers ago, with reverence.
You can't blame *this* one on the Mafia. Is
it the C.I.A. again? Did they *really*
ax Kennedy? The roots of my teeth, my hair
tauten as I think of it. Then I hear the
grasses growing in the blue wind over
Wounded Knee, Ravensbruck, My Lai; voices.

Voices with plans to solve the fuel shortage,
but millions of these same voices will run their
air-conditioners full-blast this summer, snug
in First Class of SSTs, no second thoughts,
will buy that brand new snowmobile for the kids.
"We need a world grain bank in the event of
famine." Will this famine stop at seven years?
And now the voices start to sound familiar.
Athletes stranded in the Andes eat each other
to survive, with reverence. We find ourselves
appalled at this, because we'd do the same thing.
We recall Biafra, where soldiers were sold
for meat while their eyes still burned with life. Do you
remember what happened at Donner Pass, friend?
Did you ever think of giving up this meat?

I think of the young men I've met in prisons,
murderers, who know what it's all about. My
primal fear of them, then looking into their
eyes and seeing they were somehow cleansed of it.
A friend who backed over his two-year old son.
His polished shoes next to the window out which
he leapt. Of one man, so wise and beatific,
who hadn't seen the moon in four years. Asked the
warden, quietly, was denied permission.
But there sits Rusty Calley in his quarters,
files his fan mail, dresses for his evening stroll;
Less than a year apiece for each life *he* took.
Yes, but they were gooks, didn't value life, it
was war. If I asked you to choose would *you* be
the one to order these others' heads on pikes outside your
city hall, have Calley as commencement speaker
at your local high school, a patriotic
blush when you see him on some late-night talk show.

I move outside away from a voice I used
to hear each Sunday; Billy Graham, under
huge oaks in Texas. Yes, I too mourn for LBJ—
there was much compassion in the man, but my
brain swivels in my head when I think of how
your corporate voice is lulling us. A female

jay bounces across the snow to some seeds I've
just put out. A muscle in my thigh twitches
in Morse Code. I scream and the hills move away
from me in waves, my head is shucked like a leaf.
These voices! I've heard enough of them! Fists may
pommel me, bullets rip off the corneas
of my eyes, pop my eardrums if you will, but
I can still hear my heart, answer these voices.

Brother, with John Wayne demeanor, why are you
in knots, a stranger to your children? Sister,
in bouffant hairdo, love is not a country-
western song. I step into these words and walk
to you. In front of us a vision. A child
sits in silence, not male, not female. We can
smell the fragrant skin, the hair, the blazing eyes.
We hear our own bodies' inner workings. We
are moving somewhere inside; we remember
innocence. Rain begins to pock the puddles,
little chick mouths jerking open to the sky.
I stand here in the rain and begin to weep.

Taos, N.M.   II/III:73

Antar S. K. Mberi

NUFLO DE OLANO (WHO SAILED WITH BALBOA)

I called your moon-dried name
a cargo of salted history
out of the dark hole
of night's big boned ship
as once was called Balboa
with his imperial spirit of adventure

to touch his impregnable pale night

to touch your charcoal existence
I called

simply because we need
to know you

simply because names
with your shade of sun burning them black
were waylaid in the sealanes of US history

because breasts of hate go on sinking
sharp teeth into your dreams
saying you never laughed
with your bituminous bearded face
of the lost discoverers

because lost like lice in his thick beard
they go on maliciously boasting only of Balboa
who lived with light and waves
in his eyes, new horizons in his hands
and his infamous crimes of conquest
as he stumbled through the continent
baptizing the natives with cross
-bows, ball and blade
and the "religion" of his skin
holy as an avalanche of snow

Out of the big boned dark
hole of our past, a ship
filled with living
full as a planet
I call your name ancestor
not to chant praises
(you too are judged imperial
    how many red brothers of mine
    kissed God's bloody lips
    on your blade?)
but to know and justify your existence

I call your name of light and wave
and new horizons held captive in the eye:

Nuflo de Olano, explorer

simply because this morning
our children asked me
their names

simply because this morning
they needed to know

if history had eluded them
if coal-faced conquistadors, too
opened the corridors to the "new world"

So I called
Nuflo de Olano.

Nuflo de Olano
I called

Judith Moffett

EVENSONG

Now the Earth turns, and tilts me from the sun.
Her swirling whites and blues grow shadowy now.
Twilight. Then dusk. Soon night must fall, a crow
Sweeping strong feathers down.
This lovely leper Earth, so lovely still
She stops the heart, will never, now, get well.

Her sluggish stinking rivers flow to oily
Seas; her skies, stack-tortured, thicken daily.

Above me now—far, high, outstripping sound—
A jet's thin parallel emissions shine
Roseate with the sunset's benison;
Soften; and pillowlike are plumped by wind.
The little silvery thing,
Wasp-graceful, tilts its warheads on one wing
And turns as Earth does. Steady and serene
It draws the spreading threads out in a line.

And nearer carrion crows than this are circling
The Earth in torment. Men of Power aggress,
Plunder, wrest, blast, enkindle furnaces
And manufacture things. Our desperate darkling
Globe cannot be healed except through power;
For Progress and the GNP therefore,
Leisure, and General Prosperity,
The Earth shall surely die.

She is a living sacrifice that saves
Nothing. And though the stopwatch heart be struck
Dumb with Earth's beauty still, I see the wick
Shorten, the flame flicker. Red lancet leaves
Hurtle against my heart, against blue sky;
Now by that piercing, deepening blue I swear
To cherish life, while round me, vivid, pure,
Life licks and burns at me.

DIRGE FOR SMALL WILDDEATH

So many damp hanks of hair and feathers
horribly take the measure of my country
walking: possums, grasshoppers, snakes,
frogs and woodchucks and sparrows, overtaken
by traffic, flattened or knocked aside.
Immense, our incidental slaughter

of small wild creatures. Today
I found another skunk, mouth full
of dirt, bloated, pregnant, dead
on her back. The pavement's smeared
with violent matted fur and entrails. A faint,
lingering, unmistakable skunk-musk
clings to the road's shoulder.

Bred wise enough to crouch
or scuttle from a man on foot
loose in their territory, what beguiles
these bodies new each morning
beside roads, when they in safe darkness
emboldened by their stink
come trotting out of brush thickets
onto the hard surfaces where huge
blinding things rush upon them? What
can it mean to luckier skunks
to happen on this one: food for nothing,
defending no kits, not starved, diseased, tooth-torn,
trapped by water or fire—yet dead?

John Morgan

OUR "CIVILIZATION"

Just a scuzzy black puddle in the driveway.
All through the modern age the sense of self
has been diminishing, and on this dry morning

observe the edges of the puddle shrinking back,
leaving a residue of skum five molecules thick on the rough
surface of the blacktop, where the new Buick goes

back and forth through the day
as the wife goes out and back: to the dry-cleaner,
the hair-dresser, picks up her children

at school, her husband at the station.
Soon it is evening.
Lights on in the house and the television speaking.

I walk through the darkness and come to the puddle.
At a certain angle the half-moon
is reflected. as I totter on the edge looking down,

for this is a puddle I could fall into,
fall   deep   deep   and swim like an eel in the ocean
among the coral and the stones

and the old tires and rusted cans
which have drifted out here miles from shore
on which algae grow, and where the fry, the guppies

that I live on make their homes.
In the vast ocean I slither along the bottom
through the cold muck, a dark electric thing

of which the children are not taught at school,
of which the television makes no mention.
Then, after the children have been put to bed

one by one the lights in the house click off
and the shrunken puddle fills up the darkness.
I swim through windows and doors

and populate the house with dreams.
I am a needle swimming through the eyes of dreamers,
each soul in the house a patch sewn into a quilt.

But somewhere a child (the little girl)
has thrown her cover to the floor.
She sits up in the dark shivering and yells

yells   yells out at the sensible night.
The others rush in and say hush, it is nothing, nothing at all,
and after a while she calms herself, is consoled
(tomorrow the puddle will be gone) and sleeps.

Joan Murray

THE LOVERS

Last night
they made love
a new way:
her skirt draped
across the bed,
the delicate
white blouse
beside his suit,
the red striped tie
laid neat.
Being caught
there is no
embarrassment.

The note won't tell
what they whispered
in their ritual
to ease each other
to the bright breaking
of blood
as on the first night.
After fifty years
there was no need

to be naked
to be assured
by a hair pelt
touched
into heart grain.

Last night it was
a new position:
their love binding
their necks
to doorknobs,
razors
at their wrists
releasing
one another
to supreme escape.

Far away
in the Arctic
the aged
wander snowdeep
to the polar jaw.
In Africa
they seek uplands
and await
a predatory kiss.
Here in America
they are left behind
in cities
to make love.
For *them*
there is no
embarrassment.

Despondent from beatings and burglaries,
Hans and Emma Kable, close to eighty,
took their own lives, Bronx, New York.

AN IRISH BLESSING

For Jim

genocide
castrated nation
you cannot call it father land

I

They are frail, you think,
because they are Irish
You believe your people are a little frail
a little patsy
and a little blarney

They endear themselves in the lie
to the tunes of pipes and fiddles

But once pipes wailed
to women/like wolves in battle,
and men scorning armor
naked together in the clash
and poets ruling them all
with words and words
that could blast the frail ones
back to Britain
if their ears could comprehend such song

Down their centuries you come,
the uterus lax with wear,
you are a breast beggar
push a brother
from the nipple.
Your father gives the name:
James "supplanter",
his fifth son
planned as Peter "rock"
to be hard as Crom Cruach

but it is James/Supplanter
his own name:
He watches next year
as a brother
rips you off the breast

II

Your mother
motherless at five
rises off the land
leaves the children she raised
at five
and comes here bearing eight

There is no room
on a lap with seven
You try for a stake
close to the source,
pushed down the thigh
along the femur
to the knee
and off

Still you know your land
your mind shapes to its memory,
you know it with its life rising off its bones

know its first defenders
starved into eating
their honored dead

know its ten thousand vanquished
ripped by their roots
forced to crawl like snakes off the island,
supplanted by settlers
who crossed the Irish Sea
to bloom a cash crop on stolen land,
trample the Irish and say they have no backbone

only smiling eyes

and you know the slaves remaining
who cannot vote,
cannot own land,
not even a decent horse,
cannot educate their children

such is the law

Alive only to work
their learning lost in the church,
its doors nailed shut for centuries

III

A child
in the dark you rise by six
deliver papers
step jump roof to roof
cross landings over sleeping tramps
your nickels are brothers to your family/
hungry from fast
serve mass at seven
I watch you from a distance
tired at the start of day:
in your heavy knees
the million dead
clawing for the lost potato/
at your back the million
who turned their backs
and came
still turning and turning/
and in your eyes the mother
banger of bin lids
who today was blasted
from ten children's eyes

Your mother does not call you to the phone:
they ask for Mugs
wild Irish Mugs
bound for the Harlem
a beer case

on your shoulder
draw/stud
shoot craps
your friends shoot heroin
and people

Turning traitor
you may take your father's land
supplant him by the law

but you do not seek his land
or life

You, his namesake
worn out walking
while he drove a bus
hand me down and down and down
linoleum in your shoes
homemade haircuts,
now a lawyer, teach college,
run a drug program:

the neighbors say you are "a cop"
the sound low and familiar

IV

down so long

the little people
little people

turn your banshees
to the seacoast
and wail against

genocide
against slaves
kept down ignorant
dirty working poor

hanged drawn quartered
their tongues cut off
their language broken
into moans
that cross the sea
in jigs in reels in bars
on every corner

Who put the overalls

The Irish washwoman
the Irish bus driver
the Irish who laid the rails
the Irish who served
and served and served
to make their sons such plums
for priests and presidents,
who lose their way home
no poets left to lead them,
their fistful of fighters
interned, interred, in hiding,
passing emptied out into America
supplanted/transplanted
forgetting the debt to the land
to the last fingernail

Your father came carrying the fight,
the IRA card in his hand,
and broke himself for the bus union,
too late for his land

James/Supplanter
come after
out of time

may the land rest easy
without your step

AFTER THE MURDER OF JIMMY WALSH

Kingsbridge, Bronx;   October 9, 1975

They cannot contain the death,
it spills over into streets.
Mothers with their children
take to bottles, stones,
hurl them at passing buses.
At night the streets are littered
with hate notes scrawled on loose leaf.

The anger, the pain is cutting in:
everyone steps aside for the body.
He is a boy fifteen,
he is everyone's son and daughter,
he is the private hell of
blacks, whites, hispanics
who rise at our meeting to testify:
He is the raped wife of the Greek
who works nights at the corner diner/
He is the murdered child of the man
who breaks his broken English sobbing
that he will protect *sus niños*.

The dead one is buried
under lost jobs and voices
where minds are shattered, squeezed
together into this last corner
of a city that believes God
has only vengeance left to grant them.
The buses pass with school boy murderers.
"Keep them out. Keep them out of here."
Some say "black" when they mean "bad":
there is a long line for blood.

"It is a white neighborhood"
only in a rent gouger's lie.
Escape to this place wearing your color
and find the pain is all the same:

at last you find equality
working hard to keep your kids alive,
they put hope in chains and bats,
talk of "turf" as if it were their future.
Here boys are shot from bus windows,
their mothers killed in hallways:
The *Times* called this "Blood Country"
even before the stabbed boy left the bus.

His death stings the weary eyes:
some see it sharp only in black and white,
they rock buses wailing "our son is dead".
Two thousand people empty into the nightmare
to pass time while their city dies.
From windows they shout,
"Leave our buses. We are not murderers"/
From sidewalks they chant "Jimmy Walsh",
and never hear each other's truth.

Ed Ochester

FOR REFUGIO TALAMANTE

because in Argentina
cattle prods sputter and crack
with the secret police
against her daughter
Olga. Because Olga
has such deep eyes
and strong hands. Because
she says "8 to 10 men
in the room and I

was naked and tied
to a bed. I was stronger.
They needed 10 men
and an electric machine
against me
because I was stronger."
Because the State Dept.
is indifferent,
because it pays
the torturers.
Because thousands speak up.
Because thousands cry out.
Because Olga has such strong hands.
Because she is flown to California.
Because Refugio
cooks for their friends.
Because Refugio's hands
work as she talks.
Because Refugio says
"I ask myself
why does a person
suffer so much,
bear so much?
Because the more one suffers
the more one struggles
and then the less one sorrows.
This I have learned
from my daughter."

KILLING RABBITS

Bend the neck back quickly
until it snaps,
cut off the head
close behind the skull.
Hang the carcass by a rear foot to bleed.
Skinning's easy: cut off the three loose feet
and tail with pruning shears, slit the fur

along the rear legs to the root of the tail
and pull off the pelt like a glove.
Cut through the skin of the belly,
the guts spill out of their little tub.
(I knew a man could clean a rabbit
by snapping the slit carcass like a whip).

This is ugly. You wouldn't do it,
though you like to eat meat,
fat gravy made with the blood of steers,
sausages stuffed with the brains of pigs.

You were always delicate,
averting your eyes in Florida
as your Buick purred by the migrants,
ten people in a tin-roof hut.
You were happy, years ago, when you got
to the bridge without crossing Harlem.
Even the steelworkers flowing like a dark river
oppress you; you ride past J & L
forcing your hands
to leave the windows open.
In the supermarket you shrink
from blood-water in the plastic trays,

though your appetite is healthy.
In the silence of your well-policed rooms
your capped teeth flash and tear flesh.

TOWARD THE SPLENDID CITY

All paths lead to the same goal:
to convey to others what we are.
                    —Neruda

This is why in the wormpaths
of my solitary life
I want to grow cabbages,
with my thumb brush away
the tiny weeds, amaranth and purslane.

Do this early in the morning
before the birds are weary
or the sun bakes clay.
I remember how my grandmother
gave gifts of tomatoes and cucumbers,
picked the vegetables as the sun rose
and left them by doors
of silent houses.

If I could cultivate and water
the hearts of my children
I would do it,
my daughter strong and delicate
as fennel,
my son tough and moody as onions
upright in their solitude.

But there one works by indirection
in the strong heat of afternoons.
One hints and jokes,
loves by discussing the magnitude of suns
with a drink in one's hand,
or thudding softballs through the heavy air.

And in Pittsburgh,
where the blood of lost workers
haunts the soil beneath the pavement,
one afternoon I found under my office door
an anonymous note: "I love you."

Because we live this way we dream
of a whole people walking together
through their fields,
the work in common,
bodies touching,
eyes clear.

This is where one's fingers speak.
And in the long rest after labor
a voice works through the fall streets
to meet its lover
beneath the white ring of ice.

Peter Oresick

FAMILY PORTRAIT 1933

In the center my grandfather sits
a patriarch, a boy on his knee
and progeny surrounding. His face says
this is my contribution, but the lips wanting
reassurance. My grandmother is a trunk
of a woman three children wide,
her face stern and unfathomable.

While they are stiff and attentive,
I would like to speak.
Father, I'd say, you are twenty
now, but will lease your body out
to machines like the man did
on whose shoulder you rest your hand.
And after forty years you'll say
"I'm just an old man smoking cigarettes
in the cellar, fixing radios."
Uncles, aunts, I cannot keep track
of you. Live.
Grandfather, grandmother, don't worry.
I'll be born in twenty-two years
and grow strong and bury you.
Uncle Mike, old mole,
you will bury yourself
in the anthracite fields of Pennsylvania.
Please resume now. Come unfrozen,
quickly; do what you must do.

ELMER RUIZ

Believe me,
it's like a doctor.
I go & mark
the grave to be,
put a layer of charcoal
& by morning 15 inches
of frost be completely
melt.

Kinda like an operation.
A human body's goin into it.
If you don't know where to cut,
you're not gonna have a success.
I had a sewerdigger once
wanted to see a grave.
He was impressed—
how square, how perfect!

Hear about the strike we had
in New York? The cost of funerals
they raised; they didn't want
to raise us; 20,000 bodies layin
didn't get lowered.

I will usually wear myself
some black sunglasses.
This grief I see everyday.
Believe me, it makes you turn.
Your eyes shows you have a big emotion.
Always these black glasses for me.

You, you can dig a hole
anyway they come. But a gravedigger,
well, for that you need skill.
We gotta make a nice job.

AFTER THE MOVEMENT

Reading,
weary again.
I think of Marx's eyes,
hard, indefatigable pepper-
corns.

Outside, sprinklers
whir & spin, persistent
as a March of Dimes
volunteer. *I give, I give.*
These books are sunlight trapped

in clear jars—pulsing light.
A man could live fishing or
berrying. Some life. No,
I want to be the squirrel bounding
across high-voltage wires

while rollerskates, Buicks
rage below, banged up & green.
Moonlight: lead me over.

Gregory Orr

BEGGAR'S SONG

See this seed? Food
for a week. That cowskull
in the pasture? Backroom
where the brain was:
spacious hut for me.

Small then, and smaller.
My desire's to stay alive
and be no larger
than a sliver
lodged in my own heart.

And if the heart's a rock
I'll whack it with this tin
cup and eat the sparks,
always screaming, always
screaming for more.

SONG OF THE INVISIBLE CORPSE IN THE FIELD

And still I lie here,
bruised by rain, gored
by the tiny horns
of sprouting grass.

Meanwhile I hum
the song of spiders
drawing, across the dulled
mirrors of my eyes, accurate
maps for the spirit's quest:
always death at the center
like Rome or some oasis
toward which all paths tend.

I am the absence
under your feet, the pit
that opens, toothed with dew.

Marge Piercy

THE LOW ROAD

What can they do
to you? Whatever they want.
They can set you up, they can
bust you, they can break
your fingers, they can
burn your brain with electricity,
blur you with drugs till you
can't walk, can't remember, they can
take your child, wall up
your lover. They can do anything
you can't stop them
from doing. How can you stop
them? Alone, you can fight,
you can refuse, you can
take what revenge you can
but they roll over you.

But two people fighting
back to back can cut through
a mob, a snake-dancing file
can break a cordon, an army
can meet an army.

Two people can keep each other
sane, can give support, conviction,
love, massage, hope, sex.
Three people are a delegation,
a committee, a wedge. With four
you can play bridge and start
an organization. With six
you can rent a whole house,
eat pie for dinner with no
seconds, and hold a fund raising party.

A dozen make a demonstration.
A hundred fill a hall.
A thousand have solidarity and your own newsletter,
ten thousand, power and your own paper;
a hundred thousand, your own media,
a million, your own country.

It goes on one at a time,
it starts when you care
to act, it starts when you do
it again after they said no,
it starts when you say *We*
and know who you mean, and each
day you mean one more.

THE INSIDE CHANCE

Dance like a jackrabbit
in the dunegrass, dance
not for the release, no
the ice holds hard but
for the promise. Yesterday
the chickadees sang *fever,*
fever, the mating song.
You can still cross ponds
leaving tracks in the snow
over the sleeping fish
but in the marsh the red
maples look red
again, their buds swelling.
Just one week ago a blizzard
roared for two days.
Ice weeps in the road.
Yet spring hides
in the snow. On the south
wall of the house
the first sharp crown

of crocus sticks out.
Spring lurks inside the hard
casing, and the bud
begins to crack. What seems
dead pares its hunger
sharp and stirs groaning.
If we have not stopped
wanting in the long dark,
we will grasp our desires
soon by the nape.
Inside the fallen brown
apple the seed is alive.
Freeze and thaw, freeze
and thaw, the sap leaps
in the maple under the bark
and although they have
pronounced us dead, we
rise again invisibly,
we rise and the sun sings
in us sweet and smoky
as the blood of the maple
that will open its leaves
like thousands of waving hands.

Alberto Ríos

BELITA

The faces and the hands of her grandchildren
had grown too big to fit through her eyes.
She learned to keep bowed her head
because fingers and ankles she could recognize

and faces she could not, not even her own
which fit her now like a wrinkled handkerchief,
like the brown, unlaundered, unironed handkerchief
she kept always in her hands because her grandchildren
had given it to her, had allowed her to own
some part of them, a larger part than her eyes
would have allowed; she could recognize
in her hands the face from her head
better than in a mirror, and her head
felt lighter without eyes, or ears, and the handkerchief
she massaged constantly showed her how to recognize
clearly why not one of her grandchildren
would touch her; she could feel their eyes
also with her fingers, and they were like her own,
afraid of looking, and their lips were like her own,
afraid of speaking, and she was kissed only on the forehead
because of this, and with her fingers that were eyes
she felt afraid, again, again, crushing the handkerchief
because these were the children of her children
and in them she could not fail to recognize
herself, trying nervously, trembling, not to recognize
death, how it had taken her name, Belita, for its own.
She remembered her friends suddenly as children,
how they had played Death like this because ahead
only dinner waited for them, how each took a handkerchief
and pulled it slowly over the mouth, the nose, the eyes.
Now it was her turn, and quickly her own eyes
closed; in her short life she had learned to recognize
how a sheet was like a handkerchief
and how both could be her own, and yet not her own,
how each covered easily the length of her head,
how the pennies put on her eyes balanced like children.
But those eyes are not her own.
She cannot recognize any longer the little head,
covered now by that handkerchief, kissed by the children.

THE MAN WHO NAMED CHILDREN

Panfilo's head was shaped awkwardly
so that his mother would let out
one side of his hat.
He prayed for himself
and confessed this, finally
to the priest, Father Torres
who recognized Panfilo's voice
in the confessional and said
it was all right.
The priest was there
when Panfilo was born,
when his mother almost died
and needed extreme unction.
Panfilo remembered being scared.
He was taken wrapped in a blanket
to his father who wanted a son.
But this is ugly! said his father
and held him up by the lightbulb
so the other men could see.
I will name him Panfilo
he decided, and from my corner
I remember seeing as the men
looked down at their hands
and said to Panfilo's father *yes*,
each in his turn.

Del Marie Rogers

WAR REQUIEM

The restless water of sound,
a community of singers, one song,
one harsh voice,
the souls of the dead flow over our hands . . .

the fast pick-up truck on a winter morning
is full of shaking branches, wet, piied high, precarious,
hanging out behind the truck,
cut off, hurtling forward in the cold sky.

SLEEP

I don't want to open my eyes again
but I don't want to die,
to be cold forever,
I want a tree
to grow out of my head and live
with power, to live sightlessly, green.

I want to lie down
near the horizon's perfect ring,
in the blurred sky.

If only human touch
were enough: there are thousands of hands.
The trees live beyond us
burning straight upward.

James Scully

ESPERANZA

The bony black face
of Esperanza

archaic face
of blood work, chicken
slaughter, pinfeathers, salted carcasses,
of hands condemned to glow
in cold dreamless water,
cold cement
stopping the feet dead,

the look of work
and strike, one more
picket with a slag foot rhythm
that says, we won't kill ourselves,
we can walk this line forever,
or what amounts to forever . . .

Esperanza is sick of forever.

On the strict iron
of the fire escape, she bristles
like chilblains in sunlight
resting her bones against the warm brick wall.

Against the world, which is
legal and Anglo, she yanks
a lavender vinyl collar across her face.
Not like an ostrich, but an old opera.
They want her soul her bread
her food stamps, welfare
check, slave pay,

her 30 dollar a week
union dole.
Her man, her coat.
Even at night
she pulls the night over her head.
Even her cunning
gets carried away
on the wings of her innocence.

The cold damp air
is killing her.
She's picking up what she can,
flying back
to Puerto Rico,
wherever it is—

a thin black bird
good morning'd and fed,
have a pleasant trip
as never before, never again,
in the belly lap
of a huge silver bird . . .

coming down into
factory clouds of sunset chemicals,
flecks of ash,
the queasy
blue wrinkled bay water,
skimming and overshooting
rows of stunted
pineapples withering in the field

a few shreds
of fading color,
the same earth
she had come from, gone to, and left.

A swollen superport
rose from the sea, draining the sea.
A third of the women had been sterilized.

Limousines
sped past vacant lots. Gardenias.

A mountain of nickel,

gouged face . . .

Esperanza
shivered to bone
in the throat of restaurants,
in plump bodega hearts,
and in the labyrinth of refineries
—high flying
    torches
        burning off the night—
in the sublime
filaments of computers
that could not swallow her,
and cannot spit her out.

Now all the hand-slapped guitars
put on
smiles of glass.
They have a mouthful
of sharp dark bird, petty
thievery, acrid
envy;
Esperanza
fills their mouths with blood.

. . . Unborn skies
come to stare: at broken
palm fronds, broken words,
at what seem to be
hands
wrung like flags of shame.

To stare, and wonder how so much
wealth made so much poverty
so much alone,

how so much misery
made Esperanza

who expected
nothing

scavenge in the cracks
of her own hands.
This
thing that existed only

to bury her face in the dust of Puerto Pobre.

ENOUGH !

And now they are no longer
man and father,
woman and mother,
but 2
workers in old age:
heroic and used-up
as smoldering rags.

Her, she's
a tiny cell of light
—40 watts, say,
against 3 backyards
and one small, dirty sidestreet—
in an immense night.

She dreams no more
than the dog, Toro,
chained to the back porch.

Six days she goes
out into the marbled mist
of streetlamps, dawn, dripping trees,
the sky
with its wisp of moon.

Sundays she sleeps.

Across the city, by the harbor,
the cable coiling
machines she tends
are not what they are,
but the oily roar
of her horizon.
An end.

And him?
Back from the hospital
he sits in the kitchen.
His brain scatters
wishes
and insights, like fireflies
through the terrible spring night

only to say
how dark it is,

how 38 years
boxing chemicals and beakers,
grinding glass,
add up
to $57.60 a month
for life: enough
for dog food, cheap
stupefying wine,
rest beyond belief.

It is more
than enough.

THE DAY OF THE NIGHT

The day of the night
they arrested Fernando:
I'm lounging on a bench,
among retired old men
and purple flowers
in the Plaza de Armas.

A one-legged man
rolls his sleeves up
and hums: over
an iron water bubbler
bubbling over
his hands and forearms.
Having dropped his crutch
he's washing away.
The wornout
blue of his shirt
is gray as the overworked sky.
He could be a cloud
       blue
bird with spindly legs,
standing, one leg
more or less straight,
the other tucked up
under its belly:
tossing a splat of drops
off, onto the packed dirt
under a huge leafy palm
that droops and crests
—but motionless—
in carbon monoxide
it can live with,
the way an oasis
lives with desert.

He will stand
72 hours, without
a thing to eat,

a black
hood over his head.

If we had wings, roots, petals
we would not be men.

INNOCENCE

      Like any brute, to have a soft heart.

To be the last benevolent despot
or revolutionary without arms.

Imprisoned by Bonaparte
to embrace Sade,

to spit out, as he did,
'At least *I* never killed anyone'

To have thought that good
or good enough.

Like any beast, to have dreamed
murder begins or ends

in flesh and blood.

So. To have sought like a dog
panting with peace and love

Or bought a man or woman
however thrilled or willing the ruin

To have used a piece of human.

To didn't mean to do it
and be sincere.

You held yourself pure
regardless.

You thought you were the motto?
You were the money.

And once upheld the Universal Declaration of Human Rights,
forgetting to feed the cat.

A man and woman of principle
a real shit

to have been wishful,
for ever and ever

To have sung your starry ideal
lulling as an alibi

Evening news rocked like a bedtime story

so awful and graceful
it had no moral.

You had been above all
impartial

Every question, like genocide,
had at least two sides

every question a burning answer.

You wept at the blood,
washed and wept

for the good it did.

Bitter at the end,
guilt was your pride and joy

because you were shameless.
You had no sense of shame.

You were no solution.
You were you.

My heart went out to you
as an executioner,

it did what it had to do.

You could not, could not tell
my heart from my hand.

R. T. Smith

WHAT BLACK ELK SAID

It was in the Moon when the Cherries Turn Black.
We cut birch saplings and
packed our tipis on travois
and followed the Bison Wind to the banks of the Rosebud.
But that was not a good year.
The Arapahoes we called Blue Clouds
attacked our hunting parties under the Bitten Moon,
and the leaves fled early.
In that hungry winter some say snow reached
the ponies' withers. The elk were hard
to find and many of our people forgot
to slit bone masks and went snowblind.
Some of the bands got lost for awhile. Some died.
I think it was that winter when a medicine man

named Creeping came among us curing
the snowblinds. He packed snow across their eyes
and sang the sacred song from his dream.
Then he would blow on the backs of their heads
and sing *hey hey hey hey* and they would see.

It was about the dragonfly
whose wings wear eyes that he sang,
for that was where he claimed his power lay.
We, too, spoke to the snow of dragonflies,
and soon the deep patches melted
and the hunters brought us fresh meat.
Creeping left one night, slung on a pony drag.
Some say he was a man of much crazy.
I thought so too, but the next summer
I had my vision of giants slanting down like arrows
from clouds. They sang a sacred song of the elk
speaking with the sacred voice.
The next year was the good year.
A song was singing me.

Bradford Stark

ALWAYS MODERN TIMES

The history of the city
is a history of congestion

and despair.

Look around you.

What is there but plaster
                    falling

and stores to clean your laundry.

Even the rich are fooled.

    In his treatise
the scholar can note only

the invention of the watercloset in 1596
as crucial.

The history of the city
is a history thriving

on the intimate processes which are used to describe it.

It is always modern times.

Quincy Troupe

THESE CROSSINGS, THESE WORDS

For Pablo Neruda (1904-1973)

where will they take us to
these crossings
over rivers of blood-stained words
syllables haphazardly thrown together
as marriages that fall apart
in one day

we have come this far in space
to know nothing of time
of imprisoning distance travelled scab-fleshed
hobos passed cloning
we have most times asked nothing
of mirrors reflecting our own shattering

passing us as lava smoldering in streets

in our red eyes the guillotine
smile of the hangman
a time-bomb ticking for our hearts
the brain an item bought like so much gooey candy
the laugh a razor's flash
party time juba
of My Lai's sickening ritual

american as elvis presley's drugged days
dead now as his stolen black rhythms
& the blood-scarred wind
whipped rag blue squared off with stars
that are silver bullets
& pin-striped with bones of mythologized peppermint
will not hide the corpse-lynched history hanging there
twisting slowly
as a black man's creaking body
screaming through soft magnolia air
over a tear-stained bride's veil
breeze blown & fluttering
as a flopping fish
in a gesture of surrender

we have come all this distance in darkness
bomb-flashes guiding our way
speaking of love / of passions instantly eclipsed
to find this corpse of freedom hung & machine gunned
for cross fertilizing blood wearing a name
beneath a simple word
(& what do we know who have not gone there in truth
of the roots of these flames burning at river-crossings
the crossbones of our names signaling connecting

rivers of blood beautiful as fusing
coltrane solos?)

& there are times when we see
celluloid phantoms of mediarized lovers
crawling from sockets of cracking up skeletons
born in cameras & t.v. screens
we think are ourselves

times still when we stand here
anchored to silence by terror
of our own voice & of the face revealed
in the unclean mirror shattering the image
of our sad-faced children
dragging anchors of this gluttonous
debauchery & of this madness
that continues to last

THE DAY DUKE RAISED; May 24th, 1974

For Duke Ellington

1.
that day began with a shower
of darkness calling lightning rains
home to stone language
of thunderclaps shattering the high
blue elegance of space & time
a broken-down riderless horse
with frayed wings
rode a sheer bone sunbeam
road down into the clouds

2.
spoke wheels of lightning
spun around the hours high up
above those clouds duke wheeled
his chariot of piano keys

his spirit now levitated from flesh
& hovering over the music of most high
spoke to the silence
of a griot shaman/ man
who knew the wisdom of God

3.

at high noon the sun cracked
through the darkness like a rifle shot
grew a beard of clouds on its livid bald
face hung down noon sky high
pivotal time of the flood-deep hours as duke
was pivotal being a five in the nine
numbers of numerology
as his music was the corssroads
cosmic mirror of syncopated gri-gri

4.

so get on up & fly away duke
bebop slant & fade on in strut dance swing riff
float & stroke those tickling gri-gri keys
those satin ladies taking the A train up to harlem
those gri-gri keys of birmingham
breakdown sophisticated
ladies mood indigo
get on up & strut across gri-gri
raise on up your band's waiting

5.

thunderclapping music somersaulting
clouds racing across the blue deep wisdom
of God listen it is time for your intro duke
into that other place where the all-time great band is
waiting for your overture duke it is time duke
time for the Sacred Concert duke
time to make the music of God
duke we are listening for your intro
duke let the sacred music begin

H. L. Van Brunt

LUMIÈRE

The cathedral window was a cliché
she hardly noticed,
and what she saw
of the stairs for years
was the carpet wearing thin.

Light now
is the only visitor.
The nurse leaves the door ajar,
and the pillows propped up high
from morning till afternoon.

She watches first the leaded glass
begin to glow,
and then the whole
body of light
leans toward the right.

It seems to grip the balustrade—
as a waiter might, carrying a tray;
and so carefully and slowly climbs
the stairs, he takes all afternoon
bearing up the light.

ON THE DEATH OF NERUDA

Out of a vacancy of sky,
out of pure atmosphere,
colorless and unalloyed, the wind
without history or beginning

is all at once here—
shredding the last leaves from limbs,
forcing its presence on everything.
Sometimes I think the wind
(the unsteady seething way
it beats across these fields)
bears the mumblings of confused
millions who have starved
humbly, standing in lines—
that they who were denied
the affections of the times
hold to one another
in a world behind the wind—
that somehow they survive,
heard
but never understood.
We hold our arms,
not from the cold
but out of fear
of the unknown.

WALKING

I sing the body electric . . . —Whitman

Trees with
leaves of rain
shine
down long rows of streets.
Footsteps pound. From heels a curious
surging of the nerves
floods in steady shocks. Hands
feel electric. Eyes
glow more than a cat's. Body,
organic as a tree,
with perfect faith in molecules,
would walk to the end of the world—
singing blood's syllables.

Alice Walker

ON STRIPPING BARK FROM MYSELF
For Jane, who said trees die from it

because women are expected to keep silent about
their close escapes I will not keep silent
and if I am destroyed (naked tree!) someone will please
mark the spot
where I fall and know I could not live
silent in my own lies
hearing their "how *nice* she is!"
whose adoration of the retouched image
I so despise.

No. I am finished with living
for what my mother believes
for what my brother and father defend
for what my lover elevates
for what my sister, blushing, denies or rushes
to embrace.

I find my own
small person
a standing self
against the world
an equality of wills
I finally understand.

Besides:

My struggle was always against
an inner darkness: I carry within myself
the only known keys
to my death—to unlock life, or close it shut
forever. A woman who loves wood grains, the color yellow

and the sun, I am happy to fight
all outside murderers
as I see I must.

LIGHT BAGGAGE

*For Zora, Nella, Jean**

there is a magic
lingering after people
to whom success is merely personal.
who, when the public prepares a feast
for their belated acceptance parties,
pack it up like light baggage
and disappear into the swamps of Florida
or go looking for newer Gods
in the Oak tree country
of Pennsylvania.
Or decide, quite suddenly, to try nursing,
midwifery, anonymous among the sick and the poor.
Stories about such people
tell us little;
and if a hundred photographs survive
each one will show a different face.
someone out of step. alone out there, absorbed;
fishing in the waters of experience
a slouched back against the shoulders
of the world.

*Zora Neale Hurston, Nella Larson, and Jean Toomer wrote and published
their best work during the twenties and thirties. At some point in their careers
each of them left the "career" of writing and went off seeking writing's very
heart: life itself. Zora went back to her native Florida where she lived in a one-
room cabin and raised her own food; Jean Toomer became a Quaker and
country philosopher in Bucks County, Pennsylvania; and Nella Larson, less
well known than either Hurston or Toomer, became a nurse.

THREATENED

Threatened by my rising need
he writes
he is afraid
he may fail me
in performance.
But—I tell him—
I have failed
all my life—
only with you
do I nearly succeed.
My heart—which I feel
freezing a bit each day
to this man—nonetheless
cries: Don't leave her!
Don't go! She is counting
on you!
When we talk about it
nothing to still my fear
of his fear
is said

it is this fear
that now devours
desire.

Jiri Wyatt

US

I have just realized the leaves
the boulders the grass the wildflowers
can witness anything.

Under the branches and the clouds a child
steps on a bamboo stick—which explodes
and her foot soars into the same blue.

A child bleeding to death in the heat
is unnatural, though nature witnesses.

Anyone may hang from a tree
or burn there, blackening
like a marshmallow. The tree
hasn't eyes ears or
mouth and will not weep
when seared, though it breathes.
The breath of trees also composes
the air. We have that in common.

Some would find comfort
in the seasons or in a flower
feeding on death. I do not.
I look to my friends for comfort.

Yet, blood runs down these slopes like spring snow,
streams of our human blood.
We are a spectacle to the hills and the wildflowers—
though boulders will not turn
should we no longer afflict one another.
This has to do with men and women,
it depends on us.

Al Zolynas

THE ZEN OF HOUSEWORK

I look over my own shoulder
down my arms
to where they disappear under water
into hands inside pink rubber gloves
moiling among dinner dishes.

My hands lift a wine glass,
holding it by the stem and under the bowl.
It breaks the surface
like a chalice
rising from a medieval lake.

Full of the grey wine
of domesticity, the glass floats
to the level of my eyes.
Behind it, through the window
above the sink, the sun, among
a ceremony of sparrows and bare branches,
is setting in Western America.

I can see thousands of droplets
of steam—each a tiny spectrum—rising
from my goblet of grey wine.
They sway, changing directions
constantly—like a school of playful fish,
or like the sheer curtain
on the window to another world.

Ah, grey sacrament of the mundane!

LIVING WITH OTHERS

For Arlie

Yesterday, I discovered my wife
often climbs our stairs on all fours.

In my lonely beastliness,
I thought I was alone,
the only four-legged climber, the forger
of paths through thickets to Kilimanjaro's summit.

In celebration then, side by side,
we went up the stairs on all our fours,
and after a few steps
our self-consciousness slid from us
and I growled low in the throat
and bit with blunt teeth my mate's shoulder and
she laughed low
in her throat,
and rubbed her haunches on mine.

At the top of the stairs
we rose on our human feet
and it was fine and fitting somehow;
it was Adam and Eve rising
out of themselves before the Fall—
or after; it was survivors on a raft
mad-eyed with joy
rising to the hum of a distant rescue.

I live for such moments.

TWO CHILDHOOD MEMORIES

I remember my first gun
and my first tangerine.
My father said never
point a gun at a live thing.
I was five and it was my first
gun and besides it was a toy.
I was five and I knew that.
So, I pointed the gun
at my father, at my mother.
It was a big black gun
and it wobbled a lot.
When I pulled the trigger
it went "click,"
and I think my father died.
What I remember about the tangerine
is how easily the skin came off.

THE INCUBATION

Caught Jupiter, that old benefic,
and his moons
on the Today Show this morning—
Ganymede, Io, Callisto, Europa—untold miles away
in my dining room
while I ate a waffle and yogurt before work.

There they are again, full color
on the front page
looking like someone's notion
of abstract pizza
(for all that scientists can tell us,
something out there, after all,
made of cheese).

Outside, it's early spring in Southern California,
the third day of a Santa Ana
after much rain and flooding:
three days blazing up in a glory
of new beginnings.
Who's to say this isn't the first Wednesday
of the first week of Creation?

I get into my '68 VW
with its 175,000 miles on the odometer
(this morning, the distance from Voyager One to Jupiter)
and drive off through the weird suburban
universe into the flow of the freeway

under an impossibly blue sky.

In the parking lot,
I step out of my car for the first time—
like the first robin of spring
stepping out of the shells
of the only life it's never known.

Biographical sketches

AI: Born Florence Anthony, Ai is a native of Tucson, Arizona. She has a B.A. in Japanese language and literature from the University of Arizona and an M.F.A. in writing from the University of California at Irvine. Her second collection, *Killing Floor*, was the 1978 Lamont Poetry Selection. She and her husband, the poet Lawrence Kearney, live in Stony Brook, New York.
  Cruelty. Houghton Mifflin, 1973.
  Killing Floor. Houghton Mifflin, 1979.

JODY ALIESAN: "Born April 22, 1943 in Kansas City, Missouri; grew up in Kansas, Missouri, Texas, and in an oil refinery town in Southern California which I escaped to go to school first in L.A. and then in Massachusetts. After that I taught at Miles College, a black school in Birmingham, Alabama, worked on the staff of the National Vietnam Moratorium Committee in Washington, D.C. and Chicago, and then found home here in Seattle, where I worked in women's organizations. Other places important to me: my grandfather's farm in Kansas; the North Frisian Islands (in the North Sea, off the border between Denmark and Germany), where I wandered for part of a year listening to stories."
  Soul Claiming. Mulch Press, 1975.
  as if it will matter. The Seal Press (533 11th East, Seattle, WA 98102), 1978.

TERESA ANDERSON: Of Midwestern heritage, Teresa Anderson (born 1944 in Kansas) lives in San Antonio, where she is a poet-in-the-schools. She translated the authorized American edition of Pablo Neruda's *A Call for the Destruction of Nixon and Praise for the Chilean Revolution* (West End Press, 1980), and her poetry has appeared in various magazines and anthologies, including *New Poets: Women* (Les Femmes, 1976).
  Speaking in Sign. West End Press (Box 697, Cambridge, MA 02139), 1978.

BRUCE BENNETT: Born in Philadelphia on March 8, 1940, Bruce Bennett received his doctorate from Harvard, and has taught at Oberlin, Wellesley, and Wells. He was a cofounder and an editor of both *Field* and *Ploughshares*. Among the publications in which his poetry has appeared are *The New York Quarterly, Poetry, Pequod, The Nation,* and *The Ardis Anthology of New American Poetry*.
  Coyote Pays a Call. Bits Press (Cleveland), 1980.

BERNADINE: Born of labor
        I live of struggle
        With a family of millions who do the same
        And from whom I have learned
  It Begins Softly. Women for Racial and Economic Equality (New York), 1980.

MEI-MEI BERSSENBRUGGE was born in Peking, China in 1947, grew up in Massachusetts, and now lives in a rural town in northern New Mexico. She has an M.F.A. from Columbia University. Her play *One Cup, Two Cups* was performed in New York and Seattle in 1979.
  Summits Move with the Tide. Greenfield Review Press, 1974.
  Random Possession. I. Reed Books (2140 Shattuck Avenue, Room 311, Berkeley, CA 94704), 1979.

DOUGLAS BLAZEK: "I was born in Chicago 1941. Lived in and around there until I was 25, when I moved to San Francisco, then quickly on to Sacramento, where I've been for a decade-plus now in delicious obscurity, relatively. I have no college degrees, received no literary grants or awards, and have done no teaching or anything else that is considered by university-bred culture moguls as a mark of distinction. I have devoted myself to my family and my poetry."

All Gods Must Learn to Kill. Analecta Press, 1968.

Skull Juices. Twowindows Press, 1970.

Flux & Reflux. Oyez, 1970.

Exercises in Memorizing Myself. Twowindows Press (distributed by: Serendipity Books, 1790 Shattuck Avenue, Berkeley, CA 94709), 1976.

Edible Fire. Morgan Press (1819 N. Oakland Avenue, Milwaukee, WI 53202), 1978.

OLGA BROUMAS: Born in Syros, a Cyclades island, on May 6, 1949, Olga Broumas grew up in various places in Greece and in Washington, D.C., where she "had to learn English in a state of emergency, in the last grades of grade school." She has a B.A. in architecture from the University of Pennsylvania and an M.F.A. in writing from the University of Oregon. In 1967 she held a Fulbright Travel Grant, and in 1978 a grant from the NEA. At the University of Oregon, she taught in and directed the Women's Studies Program. Presently she is poet-in-residence at Goddard College.

Caritas. Jackrabbit Press, 1976.

Beginning with O. Yale University Press, 1977.

Soie Sauvage. Copper Canyon Press, 1979.

THOMAS BRUSH: Born August 20, 1941 in Yakima, Washington, Thomas Brush "moved around continually as a kid." After taking an M.A. at the University of Washington, he drove a cab in Seattle, was a construction laborer, tended bar at a thoroughbred race track, and for the past thirteen years has taught high school English in Kent, Washington. His poems have been published in *Poetry Northwest, The Iowa Review, Shenandoah, Crazy Horse,* and *The North American Review.*

Opening Night. Owl Creek Press (Montana), 1980.

SIV CEDERING was born February 5, 1939 in Överkalix, a small town by the Arctic Circle in Sweden. After living in Sweden for fifteen years, she came to the United States. She has published two books of poetry translations, and her poetry for children, *The Blue Horse,* was published by Houghton Mifflin/Clarion Books. Currently she is completing a novel in Swedish, whose English title is *Playing in the Pig House.*

Cup of Cold Water. New Rivers Press, 1973.

Letters from Helge. (Prose poems.) New Rivers Press, 1974.

Mother Is. Stein & Day, 1975.

The Juggler. Sagarin Press, 1977.

Letters to Zakarias. (In preparation.)

HORACE COLEMAN: Born in Dayton, Ohio in 1943, Horace Coleman served with the air force in Vietnam, during which he was awarded the Bronze Star Medal. Later he earned an M.F.A. at Bowling Green University. He has been a radio talk-show host and has taught creative writing and black literature at the university level. His work has appeared in the anthologies *Demilitarized Zones, Giant Talk* (Random House), and *Speak Easy, Speak Free* (International), as well as in periodicals such as the *American Poetry Review, Hoo-Doo,* and *New Letters.* He is the father of one child and lives in Athens, Ohio.

Between a Rock & a Hard Place. Bookmark Press (5725 Wyandotte, Kansas City, MO 64113), 1978.

PHILIP DACEY was born in St. Louis on May 9, 1939, and attended the Writers' Workshop at the University of Iowa. As a Peace Corps volunteer, he taught Latin and English to secondary school students in Nigeria before moving to Southwest State University (Marshall, Minnesota), where he now teaches creative writing. Recently he completed a book-length sequence of poems about Gerard Manley Hopkins. He lives in Cottonwood, Minnesota.

How I Escaped from the Labyrinth and Other Poems. Carnegie-Mellon University Press, 1977.

The Condom Poems. Ox Head Press (414 N. 6th St., Marshall, MN 56258), 1978.

Men at Table. Chowder Chapbooks, 1979.

MELVIN DIXON (born 1950) grew up in Stamford, Connecticut, and was educated at Wesleyan and Brown. He lived in Paris for a time and has traveled to West Africa and the Caribbean. His work has appeared in the *Beloit Poetry Journal, Callaloo, Black World, Parnassus,* and Joseph Bruchac's anthology *The Next World.* He is now on the faculty at Queens College.

FRANZ DOUSKEY was born in New Haven, Connecticut, December 2, 1941, and has also lived in Mexico, the West Indies, and Tucson, where he cofounded the still-flourishing Free University. He received an M.A. from Goddard College, and has been a member of Abraham Beame's Mayor's Committee for the Aged as well as a cook for the Black Panther Breakfast Program. His poetry has appeared in the *Nation, kayak, Ironwood,* and numerous other magazines.

Indecent Exposure. New Quarto Editions (148 Orange Street, New Haven, CT 06510), 1976.

STEPHEN DUNN (born 1939) lives in Absecon, New Jersey and is poet-in-residence at Stockton State College.

Looking for Holes in the Ceiling. University of Massachusetts Press, 1974.

Full of Lust and Good Usage. Carnegie-Mellon University Press, 1976.

A Circus of Needs. Carnegie-Mellon University Press, 1978.

W. D. EHRHART was born in 1948, and grew up in Perkasie, Pennsylvania. At the age of seventeen, he enlisted in the Marine Corps and voluntarily went to Vietnam, where he earned a Purple Heart Medal and a Navy Combat Action Ribbon. After his release from active duty, he became involved in Vietnam Veterans Against the War, and coedited (with Jan Barry) *Demilitarized Zones: Veterans after Vietnam.* He has degrees from Swarthmore College and the University of Illinois at Chicago Circle, and has also been employed as a merchant seaman, forklift operator, roofer, and high school teacher.

A Generation of Peace. Samisdat Press, 1977.

Rootless. Samisdat Press, 1977.

Empire. Samisdat Press, 1978.

The Awkward Silence. Northwoods Press, 1980.

HARLEY ELLIOTT was born in 1940 in South Dakota. He grew up in Kansas, and lived in New Mexico, Colorado, and upstate New York before returning to the Midwest. He has degrees from Kansas Wesleyan University and New Mexico Highlands University, and currently teaches art at Marymount College of Kansas, in Salina. In addition, he does graphics for small press publications and his book for children, *The Tiger's Spots,* was brought out by The Crossing Press in 1977.

Dark Country. The Crossing Press, 1971.

All Beautyfull & Foolish Souls. The Crossing Press, 1974.

The Resident Stranger. Juniper Books, 1974.
Sky Heart. Pentagram Press (Markesan, WI), 1975.
The Secret Lover Poems. Emerald City Press, 1977.
Animals That Stand in Dreams. Hanging Loose Press, 1977.
Darkness at Each Elbow. Hanging Loose Press, 1981.

JOHN ENGMAN: Born March 26, 1949 in Minneapolis, Minnesota, John Engman was educated at Augsburg College and The University of Iowa. His poems have appeared in *Ironwood, Antioch Review, Iowa Review, Poetry Northwest,* and others. In addition to having been a poet-in-the-schools in Minnesota, he has worked as a waiter, laundryman, and psychiatric technician.
   Alcatraz. Burning Deck Press (71 Elmgrove Avenue, Providence, RI 02906), 1980.

SANDRA MARIA ESTEVES: Born and raised in the South Bronx, Sandra Maria Esteves studied media arts at Pratt Institute, and is a literary, graphic, and performing artist. Her poetry is included in the anthologies *The Next World, Nuyorican Poetry,* and *Ordinary Women,* which she also coedited. A recipient of a 1980 CAPS Fellowship for poetry, she has coordinated various poetry series at the New Rican Village Cultural Center in New York.
   Yerba Buena. Greenfield Review Press (Greenfield Center, NY 12833), 1980.

ALICE FULTON: Born (on January 25, 1952) and raised in Troy, New York, Alice Fulton moved to New York City after completing a writing degree at Empire State College. She has worked as a radio announcer, producer, and copywriter, and has received fellowships to The MacDowell and Millay Colonies. Currently she is studying at Cornell.
   Anchors of Light. Swamp Press (4 Bugbee Road, Oneonta, NY 13820), 1979.

ROGER GAESS: Born in the Connecticut industrial town of Waterbury, Roger Gaess spent his early years there and in England. He studied at Connecticut, Syracuse, and Columbia, and has traveled widely. During the Vietnam period he was a war resister. At various times he has worked as a packer, salesclerk, plating apprentice, and freelance editor; he guest-edited the special Walter Lowenfels issue of the *Small Press Review.* His poetry and prose have appeared in periodicals as diverse as *Ambit* (London), *The New York Times, Urthkin,* and *Poetry* (Moscow). At the moment he divides his time between New York and Litchfield County, Connecticut.

TESS GALLAGHER grew up in the logging camps of the Pacific Northwest near Port Angeles, Washington, and spent the summers of her childhood in the Missouri Ozarks. She was a journalist until she was twenty-one, and once had a job repairing fountains in the city parks of Seattle. In recent years, she has traveled frequently to Northern Ireland. Her second collection, *Instructions to the Double*, won the 1976 Elliston Poetry Award for best book of poems published by a small nonprofit press. She currently writes a column for the *American Poetry Review,* and coordinates the writing program at Syracuse University.
   Stepping Outside. Penumbra Press, 1975.
   Instructions to the Double. Graywolf Press, 1976.
   Under Stars. Graywolf Press, 1978.

BRENDAN GALVIN: Born 1938 in Everett, Massachusetts, Brendan Galvin "grew up on Cape Cod, where I still live part of each year, and whose land- and seascape, birds and animals continue to be at the center of my work." He studied natural sciences at Boston College and has a Ph.D. in English from the University of Massachusetts; presently he teaches at Central Connecticut State College. In addition to publishing several short stories and numerous reviews and critical essays on poetry, he wrote the narration for the documentary film "Massachusetts Story," which examined the offshore oil exploitation of Georges Bank. The film was nominated for three Emmys and won a first prize at the New England Film Festival.

The Narrow Land. Northeastern University Press, 1971.

The Salt Farm. Fiddlehead Books, 1972.

No Time for Good Reasons. Pitt Poetry Series: University of Pittsburgh Press, 1974.

The Minutes No One Owns. Pitt Poetry Series: University of Pittsburgh Press, 1977.

Atlantic Flyway. University of Georgia Press, 1980.

MARILYN HACKER was born on November 27, 1942 in New York City, where she resides now, with her daughter Iva, after having lived in San Francisco and London. Her first collection, *Presentation Piece,* was a Lamont Poetry Selection of the Academy of American Poets and also received the National Book Award in 1975. She is an editor of *The Little Magazine,* and teaches in the General Studies Division of Columbia University.

Presentation Piece. Viking, 1974.

Separations. Knopf, 1976.

Taking Notice. Knopf, 1980.

LAWSON FUSAO INADA (born May 26, 1938) edited *Aiiieeeee: An Anthology of Asian-American Writers* (Doubleday, 1976), and has been anthologized in *Giant Talk* (Random House) and *The Best of Yardbird* (Grove). He teaches English at Southern Oregon State College, and on January 3, 1980 was one of twenty-one poets who read at the White House for "A Salute to Poetry and American Poets." He writes, "The West Side of Fresno is where I'm from, continually coming from, and inside of me are the ABCs I was steeped in: Asian, Black, Chicano. Sure, I've travelled around some, and even spent three years in American concentration camps in California, Arkansas, and Colorado, but it's all like an extension of the West Side because wherever I am there's all that vitality and vision and laughter. And oh yes, I worked at the craft of poetry, particularly with Sensei Phil Levine, my main teacher in college. Obviously, my poetry comes out of music, extends itself from music, and that all makes sense to me because I was trying to play the bass before trying to write poetry; thus, poetry, to me, has got to say something and has got to swing—otherwise, shoot, turn the jukebox back on and let's head on over to El Jardin for some menudo."

Three Northwest Poets: Drake, Inada, Lawder. Quixote Press, 1971.

Before the War. Morrow, 1971.

The Buddha Bandits Down Highway 99: Hongo, Inada, Lau. Buddhahead Press (Santa Cruz, CA), 1979.

D. L. KLAUCK: "Born October 16, 1947 in Pittsburgh, fortunately to a great set of parents. Grew up primarily in Pittsburgh, awhile in Miami, some in Philadelphia, the Marine Corps, and finally Western State Penitentiary (PA). In my early years I was just about everything from a bouncer in a whorehouse to a quality control inspector in a bomb factory; an architectural draftsman to an armed robber. Though I attended the University of Pittsburgh, I somehow managed to learn more in the brothels and jails where real truths flourish." A recipient of three P.E.N. Writing Awards for Prisoners in both poetry and fiction, Danny Klauck serves on the Board of Directors of New York State's Alternative Literary Programs in the Schools (ALPS). *Quest/81, The Nation, The Georgia Review,* and *New England Review* are among the periodicals in which his work has appeared.

Everything else. . .. King Publications (Washington, DC), 1976.
Blood and Ashes. Thunder's Mouth Press (Oak Park, IL; distributed by: Bookslinger, Inc., St. Paul, MN), 1981.

LYN LIFSHIN grew up in Middlebury, Vermont. She has degrees from Syracuse University and the University of Vermont, has given readings and poetry workshops at numerous colleges and universities, and has published poems in a large number of small magazines and anthologies, including the breakthrough collections *Rising Tides* (Pocket Books, 1973) and *Psyche: The Feminine Poetic Consciousness* (Dell, 1973). In 1978 Beacon Press published her anthology of mother and daughter poems, *Tangled Vines.* Currently she is working on an anthology of women's journals. She lives in Niskayuna, New York.
Black Apples. The Crossing Press, 1973.
The Old House Poems. Capra Press, 1974.
Shaker House Poems. Sagarin Press, 1975.
Upstate Madonna. The Crossing Press, 1975.
Plymouth Women. Morgan Press, 1978.
Offered by Owner. (Book and record set.) The Women's Audio Exchange (Natalie Slohm Associates Inc., 49 West Main St., Cambridge, NY 12816), 1978.

LOU LIPSITZ: Born October 29, 1938, Lou Lipsitz grew up "in Brooklyn at one address." Schooled at the University of Chicago and Yale, he is now a professor of political science at the University of North Carolina. He was active in the antiwar movement of the 60s, as well as the McCarthy campaign. In the view of Hayden Carruth, "his poetry, without being programmatic, combines political and surrealistic aims, showing the influence of Neruda." He lives in Chapel Hill.
Cold Water. Wesleyan, 1967.
Reflections on Samson. kayak press, 1977.

CHARLES LYNCH: "Born (November 1, 1943) and reared in Baltimore. Attended Kenyon College (A.B.) and The City College of New York (M.A.), and completed a doctoral dissertation at New York University on the lives and work of Robert Hayden and Gwendolyn Brooks. Am presently associate professor at The Center for Labor Studies (Empire State College) in New York City. Poems in the anthologies *The Poetry of Black America: Anthology of the 20th Century* and *Celebrations: A New Anthology of Black American Poetry,* and in periodicals such as *Chelsea, Journal of Black Poetry, Yardbird Reader, Urthkin,* and *Black American Literature Forum.*"

CLEOPATRA MATHIS: Of Greek and Cherokee Indian descent, Cleopatra Mathis was born on August 16, 1947 in Ruston, Louisiana, where she lived for twenty years. She attended Louisiana Tech, Tulane University, and received her B.A. from Southwest Texas State University. Later she taught high school English for seven years, including two years in a school for the emotionally disturbed, and completed an M.F.A. in writing at Columbia University. Presently she works as a poet-in-the-schools in New Jersey. Her poetry has appeared in numerous magazines and anthologies, including *The Ardis Anthology of New American Poetry* and *Traveling America with Today's Poets.*
Aerial View of Louisiana. Sheep Meadow Press, 1979.

JUDITH MCCOMBS was born in 1939 in Alexandria, Virginia, and has lived in numerous parts of the United States and in Ghana, West Africa. In 1971 she cofounded *Moving Out,* the nation's oldest surviving feminist literary magazine. Her poetry and fiction have appeared widely in "little" and feminist magazines, and she has been anthologized in *We Become New* (Bantam) and *I Hear My Sisters Saying*

(Crowell). She now teaches wilderness literature and women's studies at the College of Art and Design (Detroit), as well as creative writing at Wayne State University.

> *Sisters and Other Selves.* Glass Bell Press (5053 Commonwealth, Detroit, MI 48208), 1976.
> *Against Nature: Wilderness Poems.* Dustbooks (P.O. Box 100, Paradise, CA 95969), 1979.

KEN McCULLOUGH: Born July 18, 1943 in Staten Island, New York, Ken McCullough has lived in all sections of the United States, as well as in Newfoundland and India. He attended the University of Delaware and the University of Iowa, taught at Montana State University and Montana State Prison, and has been writer-in-residence for the South Carolina ETV Network. His short stories have appeared in *The Iowa Review, Fantastic Stories,* and the anthology *Again, Dangerous Visions* (Doubleday).

> *The Easy Wreckage.* Seamark Press, 1971.
> *Migrations.* Stone-Marrow Press, 1973.
> *Creosote.* Seamark Press (distributed by: Richard Flamer, The Antiquarium Bookstore, 1215 Harney, Omaha, NE 68102), 1976.

ANTAR S. K. MBERI studied at Ohio University, and presently lives in New York. His writings have appeared widely, and he coedited (with Cosmo Pieterse) the anthology *Speak Easy, Speak Free* (International, 1977).

> *Bandages and Bullets: In Praise of the African Revolution.* West End Press (Box 697, Cambridge, MA 02139), 1977.
> *A Song Out of Harlem.* The Humana Press (P.O. Box 2148, Clifton, NJ 07015), 1980.

JUDITH MOFFETT was born in Louisville, Kentucky on August 30, 1942, and grew up in Cincinnati. She received a Ph.D. in American civilization from the University of Pennsylvania. In 1967-68, she was a Fulbright Lecturer at the University of Lund, Sweden. Her translations from the Swedish of Hjalmar Gullberg, *Gentleman, Single, Refined and Selected Poems 1937-1959* (Louisiana State University Press, 1979), won a Columbia Translation Prize. She presently lives in Philadelphia and teaches at the University of Pennsylvania.

> *Keeping Time.* Louisiana State University Press, 1976.

JOHN MORGAN: "I was born in New York City in 1943, grew up in the suburbs, and for a couple of summers during adolescence worked at the Peabody Museum of Natural History. I studied with Lowell at Harvard, and won the Discovery Award of The New York Poetry Center in 1969. I've taught at several colleges, and have also spent about five years 'just writing,' thanks to my wife Nancy, a musician and school teacher. For the past three years I've taught in the writing program of the University of Alaska at Fairbanks."

> *The Bone-Duster.* Quarterly Review of Literature, 1980.
> *The Border Wars.* Musk Ox Press, 1980.

JOAN MURRAY was born in New York on August 6, 1945, and grew up in the Highbridge section of the Bronx, a workingclass community on the Harlem River. Since earning her M.A. at New York University, she has taught English and writing at Lehman College of the City University of New York, and has also worked for older adult, community, and women's groups. Her poetry and fiction have appeared in several anthologies and in *The Atlantic Monthly, Harper's,* and *Ms. Magazine.* She presently lives in Buffalo.

> *Egg Tooth.* Sunbury Press, 1976.

ED OCHESTER: Born in Brooklyn, New York in 1939, Ed Ochester has lived for the past ten years on an eight-acre small farm/homestead in a coal mining area of Armstrong County, Pennsylvania, where he and his wife, Britt, grow much of their own food. At various times he has worked as a newspaper reporter, warehouse clerk, and teamster, and is now the director of the writing program of the University of Pittsburgh, as well as the editor of the University of Pittsburgh Press Poetry Series. *Coming Home,* his anthology of poems by workingclass writers, was recently issued by Stone Gargoyle Press (Atlanta).

    Dancing on the Edges of Knives. University of Missouri Press, 1973.

    The End of the Ice Age. Slow Loris Press (923 Highview St., Pittsburgh, PA 15206), 1977.

    A Drift of Swine. Thunder City Press (P.O. Box 11126, Birmingham, AL 35202), 1980.

PETER ORESICK: Born September 8, 1955 in Kittanning, Pennsylvania, Peter Oresick grew up in Ford City, Pennsylvania and currently lives in Pittsburgh. In 1977 he received a B.A. in education from the University of Pittsburgh. He has been a glassworker, a trash collector, and is now a teacher of high school English in the Pittsburgh public schools.

    The Story of Glass. West End Press (Box 697, Cambridge, MA 02139), 1977.

GREGORY ORR (born 1947) attended Hamilton College, Antioch College, and Columbia University's School of the Arts, and from 1972 to 1975 was a Junior Fellow of the University of Michigan Society of Fellows. Since then he has taught at the University of Virginia, and currently edits the poetry for the *Virginia Quarterly Review.* His wife is a painter; he writes, "We live in the countryside outside Charlottesville where the landscape is reminiscent of the Hudson River Valley where I grew up, with the Blue Ridge on the near, western horizon rather than the Catskill Mountains of my childhood."

    Burning the Empty Nests. Harper & Row, 1973.

    Gathering the Bones Together. Harper & Row, 1975.

    The Red House. Harper & Row, 1980.

MARGE PIERCY: An accomplished novelist as well as poet, Marge Piercy (born 1936) grew up in Detroit, has lived in New York, Paris, and San Francisco, and now resides in Wellfleet on Cape Cod. For a number of years she worked in various organizations of the New Left, including Students for a Democratic Society, and has been particularly active in the women's movement since 1967. She is presently on the board of Transition House, a foundation assisting battered women.

    Breaking Camp. Wesleyan University Press, 1968.

    Hard Loving. Wesleyan University Press, 1969.

    To Be of Use. Doubleday, 1973.

    Living in the Open. Knopf, 1976.

    The Twelve-Spoked Wheel Flashing. Knopf, 1978.

    Vida. (Novel.) Summit, 1980.

    The Moon Is Always Female. Knopf, 1980.

ALBERTO RÍOS: "I was born (on September 18, 1952) and grew up in Nogales, Arizona, and moved on to college sixty-five miles north, to Tucson; I've spent most of my life in these two places, and they have influenced my writing a great deal, physically and humanly. In 1980 I received a National Endowment for the Arts fellowship, and in 1981 the Walt Whitman Award for *One Night in a Familiar Room.* I am presently working for the Arizona writers-in-the-schools program, having previously taught freshman English and South American literature at the University of Arizona. In addition to poems in the *North American Review,*

Ironwood, Prairie Schooner, and others, I've also published fiction and drama. Otherwise, I mostly stay home and wash clothes."

Elk Heads on the Wall. Mango Publications, 1979.

Sleeping on Fists. Dooryard Press, 1981.

One Night in a Familiar Room. Sheep Meadow Press, 1982.

DEL MARIE ROGERS: Born in Washington, D.C., Del Marie Rogers grew up in Dallas and went to college in Waco and Austin, Texas, taking her M.A. in English from Vanderbilt. After years of living in different places, she returned in 1975 to the Dallas area, where she now is employed as a secretary to a group of auroral physicists. She was the poetry editor of *Café Solo,* and coedited, with Glenna Luschei, *I Had Been Hungry All the Years,* an anthology of contemporary women poets. Her poems have appeared in numerous magazines, and recently she completed a second book of poems, *The Sky Is Cold and Clear.*

Breaking Free. Ironwood Press (Tucson, AZ), 1977.

JAMES SCULLY: Born February 23, 1937 in New Haven, Connecticut, James Scully has lived in a variety of locations including Rome and Santiago de Chile. In 1967 he received the Lamont award for *The Marches,* and has had both a Guggenheim and an NEA fellowship. With C. J. Herington, he cotranslated Aeschylus' *Prometheus Bound* (Oxford University Press, 1975); with Maria A. Proser, *Quechua People's Poetry* (Curbstone Press, 1977); and with Maria A. Proser and Arlene Scully, Teresa de Jesús' *De Repente/All of a Sudden* (Curbstone Press, 1979). He lives in Willimantic, Connecticut and teaches at the University of Connecticut.

The Marches. Holt, Rinehart & Winston, 1967.

Avenue of the Americas. University of Massachusetts Press, 1971.

Santiago Poems. Curbstone Press, 1975.

Scrap Book. Ziesing Brothers, 1977.

May Day. Minnesota Review Press (Box 211, Bloomington, IN 47402), 1980.

R. T. SMITH: Born April 13, 1948 in the District of Columbia, R. T. Smith was raised in Griffin, Georgia and Charlotte, North Carolina, and has degrees from the University of North Carolina and Appalachian State University. Currently he teaches at Auburn University. He is a conservationist, a potter, and a carpenter.

Waking under Snow. Cold Mountain Review Press, 1975.

Good Water. Banjo Press, 1979.

Rural Route. Banjo Press, 1980.

BRADFORD STARK (born 1948) attended The City College of New York and Columbia University, and had been employed as an urban planner by several cities and consulting firms. In 1978 he received a creative writing fellowship from the National Endowment for the Arts. At the time of his death, Oct. 17, 1979, he was completing a manuscript entitled *At the Public Expense.*

An Unlikely But Noble Kingdom. The Rainbow Press, 1974.

The Burden of Time. Bellevue Press (60 Schubert St., Binghamton, NY 13905), 1976.

QUINCY TROUPE: One of the best-known poets to come out of the Watts Writers Workshop, Quincy Troupe was born on July 23, 1943 in St. Louis, Missouri, and has lived in Africa, Europe, Cuba, and Puerto Rico. A graduate of Grambling College, where he was a member of the Student Non-Violent Coordinating Committee (SNCC), he presently is an associate professor of American and Third World literatures at the College of Staten Island, City University of New York. He coedited (with Rainer Schulte) *Giant Talk: An Anthology of Third World Writings* (Random House, 1975), coauthored (with David L. Wolper) *The*

Inside Story of T̂.V.'s "Roots" (Warner Books, 1978), and is now editor of *Tne American Rag.*
> *Embryo.* Barlenmir House, 1972.
> *Snake-Back Solos.* I. Reed Books (2140 Shattuck Avenue, Room 311, Berkeley, CA 94704), 1979.

H. L. VAN BRUNT: "I grew up in Tulsa, and on a farm near the crossroads of Wingin' On, Oklahoma, and then did some more growing up in the Tulsa Children's Home, and in the State Orphanage at Pryor, Oklahoma. I lived in New York City from 1959 until 1978, but my work seems more influenced by the topography of that 20-acre farm in Oklahoma than by the potholes in Seventh Avenue."
> *Uncertainties.* The Smith, 1968.
> *Indian Territory and Other Poems.* The Smith, 1974.
> *Feral: Cow-Breath and Caw.* The Conspiracy Press, 1976.
> *For Luck: Poems 1962-1977.* Carnegie-Mellon University Press, 1978.
> *And the Man Who Was Traveling Never Got Home.* Carnegie-Mellon University Press, 1980.

ALICE WALKER was born in Georgia in 1944, attended Spelman and Sarah Lawrence Colleges, and was active in welfare rights and voter registration activities in Georgia and New York. For a time she lived with the Burgandans and the Kikuyus in Uganda and Kenya. She is the author of two novels, *Meridian* (1976) and *The Third Life of Grange Copeland* (1970); a biography, *Langston Hughes, American Poet;* and *In Love & Trouble: Stories of Black Women,* a volume of short stories. She has also taught literature and writing at several colleges, and is a contributing and consulting editor to *Freedomways* and *Ms.* magazines.
> *Once.* Harcourt, Brace & World, 1968.
> *Revolutionary Petunias.* Harcourt Brace Jovanovich, 1973.
> *Good Night, Willie Lee, I'll See You in the Morning.* Dial Press, 1979.

JIRI WYATT: Born in Slovakia in 1941, Jiri Wyatt was raised in Latin America and New York City. He was active in the antiwar movement and worked with U.S. draft-resisters in Montreal. His autobiographical essay "Against Capitulation" was published in *The Massachusetts Review,* and was reprinted in England in *Stand;* and his poems have appeared in *Poetry Review, The Southern Review, The New Yorker,* and *The Nation.* In 1978 he received a fellowship from the National Endowment for the Arts. He now lives in England.

AL ZOLYNAS: Born in Dornbirn, Austria of Lithuanian parents on June 1, 1945, Al Zolynas was raised in Sydney, Australia until the age of sixteen, when he moved with his family to Chicago. After studying at the University of Illinois and the University of Utah, he was alternately a cab driver, factory worker, and construction worker. Currently he teaches part-time at San Diego State University and United States International University.
> *The New Physics.* Wesleyan University Press, 1979.